GOING LOW

GOING LOW

How to Break Your Individual Golf Scoring Barrier by Thinking Like a Pro

Patrick Cohn, Ph.D.

Contemporary Books

Chicago   New York   San Francisco   Lisbon   London   Madrid   Mexico City
Milan   New Delhi   San Juan   Seoul   Singapore   Sydney   Toronto

Library of Congress Cataloging-in-Publication Data

Cohn, Patrick J., 1960–
    Going low : how to break your individual golf scoring barrier by thinking like a pro /
Patrick J. Cohn.
        p.   cm.
    Includes bibliographical references.
    ISBN 0-8092-9458-3 (hardcover)
    ISBN 0-07-138557-6 (paperback)
        1. Golf—Psychological aspects.   I. Title: How to break your individual golf
scoring barrier by thinking like a pro.   II. Title.
    GV979.P75 C63   2001
    796.352'01'9—dc21   00-60317

Contemporary Books

A Division of The **McGraw-Hill** Companies

1 2 3 4 5 6 7 8 9 0   VBA/VBA   0 9 8 7 6 5 4 3 2 1

ISBN 0-8092-9458-3 (hardcover)
ISBN 0-07-138557-6 (paperback)

This book was set in Sabon
Printed and bound by Maple-Vail Book Manufacturing Group

Cover design by Nick Panos
Cover photograph copyright © Michael Caulfield/AP Wide World Press

McGraw-Hill books are available at special quantity discounts to use as premiums and
sales promotions, or for use in corporate training programs. For more information, please
write to the Director of Special Sales, Professional Publishing, McGraw-Hill, Two Penn
Plaza, New York, NY 10121-2298. Or contact your local bookstore.

This book is printed on acid-free paper.

I lovingly dedicate Going Low *to our first daughter,*
Patricia A. Cohn. I hope Patti will understand why I spent so
many nights in front of the computer writing this book.
Patti will always bring joy to our lives.

CONTENTS

PREFACE

In just the last few years we have seen incredible advances in golf performance thanks to the progress made in high-tech equipment, specialized golf training programs, and golf psychology, as well as better course-management strategies used by golfers. As we continue to push the performance envelope, golfers on the pro tours are going low every week and shooting career-low and record scores. Today, golfers draw upon the knowledge of experts in golf to help them gain new insights and enhance their physical talent to make scoring breakthroughs. We could not be in a more exciting and revolutionary period in the history of golf!

Since 1998 we have witnessed three tour professional players shoot 59 and numerous others shoot scores in the low 60s. Shooting low scores is what makes professional golf so exciting for everyone in the golf world. For us mortal amateurs, just hitting that one perfect shot during a round of golf is enthralling enough to keep us coming back for more. Despite all of the mental and physical challenges of golf, golfers remain committed to playing their best. As any competitive golfer will attest, the dream is to play to one's potential, shoot a personal-low score, and win. In *Going Low*, I'm excited to share the mental game skills I teach others to help you get beyond your personal mental scoring block and set new scoring records.

For more than a decade, I have been fortunate enough to work with some of the best golfers in the world. Through my interaction with professional players, as well as amateur, junior, and college players, I've learned a lot about the psychology of peak performance and going low. Every time I observe a pro golfer shoot a low round, interview a player about the psychology of shooting low, or listen to a struggling player ask a question about golf psychology, I learn more about the game of golf, how the golfer's mind works, and the mental roadblocks that stifle success. I have discovered solutions to the most pressing problems that plague golfers and prohibit them from performing their best. In *Going Low*, I share these solutions with you.

Many golfers have asked me why it's so difficult to play well on the last nine holes of a round following a strong performance on the front nine. My answer is this: golf is mostly a mental battle. One of the major battles that challenges golfers is the struggle between their preconceived beliefs about their performance and how they actually perform on the course. Simply put, if you think you are playing better than expected, this belief will inhibit your ability to perform to your full potential.

As a sport psychologist working with golfers of all levels, I instill many of the mainstay concepts taught in sport psychology, including the Three C's (confidence, concentration, and composure). Although these mental skills are very important to success in any endeavor, golfers want to know more; they want to know how to score their best from the start to the finish of a round. That's why I've written *Going Low*. My goal is to show you how to shoot lower scores by ridding yourself of expectations, starting the round with confidence and momentum, dodging distractions, and knowing how to finish off a good round in the making. To help you further grasp and apply the information presented in *Going Low*, I use many examples from tour professionals who have shot career-low rounds to emphasize key concepts about the psychology of going low and shooting your best round.

I enjoy my work helping others succeed in sports. I especially take pride in teaching golfers at any level how to improve their performance and have more fun playing golf. I receive great gratification when I can help a young athlete successfully develop his or her game from junior through college and possibly to the professional ranks.

I would love to hear about your experiences in scoring a personal-best round. Also, if you have a puzzling question about your mental approach to golf or have a comment related to this book, please write, call, or send an E-mail. I take great pleasure in helping others simplify the complex game of golf while learning something new about the mind-set necessary to be a successful golfer.

ACKNOWLEDGMENTS

I want to thank the many players who contributed their time to talk to me about the psychology of going low. Several college, PGA, LPGA, and BUY.COM Tour players gave their time to help me formulate my thoughts about the psychology of shooting low scores. I also would especially like to thank golf writer David Gould and copyeditor Kris Evenson for their professional counsel and support during the writing of *Going Low*.

INTRODUCTION

Nothing is more exciting in golf than shooting a career-low round or witnessing a golfer going low. When you are playing great and scoring well, golf is fun, immensely satisfying, and feels second nature. To shoot a personal-best round takes a hot putter, a short game that is more precise than usual, plus a modicum of luck. In addition, it takes smart course management, complete focus on the task, and total self-composure. Somehow, the excitement stirred up by a barrier-breaking low score has to be contained—and that goes for a tour professional on the way to shooting 59 or a 20-handicapper who is breaking 90 for the first time.

Breakthroughs in Scoring

On the major professional golf tours, players seem to be shooting low more often—you hear about players shooting 62s and 63s every week. New course records are being set, tournament records are falling, and all-time PGA Tour and LPGA Tour 72-hole scoring records are being surpassed. Lower scores are due in part to improvements in equipment, course conditions, player physical training, and other player resources. At the junior levels, golfers have more access to golf courses and practice facilities, they are training for golf at earlier ages, and they have more opportunities to compete. Simply put, today's players are smarter and better equipped mentally than players a generation ago were.

Has all this low scoring on the tours proven contagious? Average handicaps don't reflect it. Average handicaps in the United States have not improved in the past 20 years even with improvements in equipment and course conditions, not to mention the great abundance of information on how to improve one's game. According to the USGA, the median handicap for men is between 15 and 16, and for women it's between 29 and 30. Fifty percent of all female golfers who keep a USGA handicap carry a handicap of 30 or higher, and only 2 percent of all golfers carry a handicap of 10 or less. Fifty-two percent of all male golfers carry a handicap of 16 or higher, and only 22 percent carry a handicap of 10 or less. These figures pertain only to an estimated five million golfers who carry USGA handicaps.

So the very good are getting better, but the average player's performance is scarcely improving. We'll examine this two-edged sword in detail later. First, let's look at what low scoring means at the top level of the game.

Theoretically, a perfect score on a par-72 course that has four par-5 holes would be 50—four eagles and 14 birdies. Why has no professional golfer even come close to shooting 50? It would take a long time and a lot of luck for someone to shoot a 50 on a par-72 course. Golf is just not that easy. Pitchers can throw a perfect game, statistically. Bowlers can bowl a perfect game. A goalie can have a perfect game with a shutout. A golfer can't shoot a perfect round. How unfair, you say. Not really—that's what makes the game of golf so interesting. No two courses are the same. No two rounds are the same. Every shot hit in golf is different, whereas in a sport such as bowling, for example, the conditions are much more finite and fixed.

I'm sure you can think of many reasons why no one has come near a perfect game of golf. I can list several besides the inherent difficulty of the game itself: (1) human error, (2) unlucky breaks, (3) personal mental barriers, and (4) unpredictable weather conditions. So many determinants influence one's golf game it is almost impossible to achieve scoring perfection. A tour pro might have a great putting round one day, or a perfect chipping game one day, or a great ball-striking round, but the possibility of all the phases of her game hitting their absolute peak on the same day is remote. David Duval had the best ball-striking round of his life when he shot 59 at the 1999 Bob Hope Chrysler Classic. I figured out that if he drained all the putts he missed (five, including his longest, a 40-footer) and sank his only two chips, Duval would have shot a 52! I think that's a lot to ask of one human.

Below is a list of players at various levels who came the closest to golf perfection.

Lowest Rounds Ever Recorded in Competition

SCPGA Boys	58—Henry Liaw*
AJGA Boys	63—Rob Beasley
AJGA Girls	62—Lee Ann Hardin*
NCAA Division I Men	62—Notah Begay
NCAA Division I Women	65—Jenny Chuasiriporn
PGA Tour	59—Al Geiberger, Chip Beck, and David Duval
Senior PGA Tour	60—Isao Aoki*
BUY.COM Tour	59—Notah Begay, Doug Dunakey*
LPGA Tour	61—Se Ri Pak**
European PGA Tour	59—Mauricio Molino, Miguel Angel Martin

Greatest Low-Scoring Rounds in Golf

You can look back in history and pick out many great rounds of golf. Most recently was Duval's final-round 59 to win the Bob Hope Chrysler Classic. Historically, you can say that Arnold Palmer's final-round 65 to win the 1960 U.S. Open, Jack Nicklaus's 65 at the 1965 Masters, and Johnny Miller's final-round 63 to win the 1973 U.S. Open are also great low-scoring rounds of golf. What defines a great round of golf? The first and most important criterion is low scoring, which becomes especially noteworthy when a player breaks a record. Where and when this round takes place is also significant;

---

*Par-70 course.
**Par-71 course.

for example, a very low round shot in a major championship commands extra respect. The 65 Arnold Palmer shot to seal his victory in the 1960 U.S. Open at Cherry Hills certainly qualifies as greatness. Winning any tournament with a super-low round, such as Duval's 59, also qualifies. Coming from behind in the last round of the tournament to win, such as Miller did in 1973, is yet another example of a great round.

All record-low-scoring rounds on the professional golf tours have to be considered great rounds, no matter what the circumstances. Certainly, the only 59s (three, to be exact) shot on the PGA Tour, the two 59s shot on the Nike Tour (now BUY.COM Tour), and the lowest 18-hole score on the LPGA Tour can all be considered great rounds. Al Geiberger was the very first player to shoot 59 in a PGA Tour event when he won the 1977 Danny Thomas–Memphis Classic. Chip Beck recorded the second 59 in PGA Tour history in the 1991 Las Vegas Invitational by making birdie on the last three holes. Beck did it on an easy par-72 course, but it still broke that psychological barrier of 60 and goes in the books as a 59. In 1998, Doug Dunakey and Notah Begay both shot 59s playing on the BUY.COM Tour; even on the so-called developmental tour, those 59s are great achievements. In 1998, LPGA Tour player Se Ri Pak shot a 10-under-par 61, the lowest score ever shot on the LPGA Tour.

Many great low-scoring rounds have not resulted in victory. Pak's 61, Beck's 59, Dunakey's 59, and Begay's 59 did not lead to wins. Certainly, low rounds that helped players win golf tournaments can be regarded as great rounds, such as Geiberger's and Duval's 59s. The strictest possible definition of a great round is one that combines dramatically low scoring with a come-from-behind victory in a major—which brings us to Johnny Miller's final-round 63 in the 1973 U.S. Open. This round is considered by many to be the best final round in a modern major championship for all the reasons just described. Other players have shot great rounds in the majors, including Greg Norman's 63 at Augusta in 1996, Nick Price's 63 at Augusta in 1986, and Helen Alfredsson's 63 in the 1994 Women's U.S. Open, but none of these players rode their stellar rounds to victory.

You can argue that a final-round 70 to win the U.S. Open in tough conditions on a tough golf course is also a great round. Payne

Stewart shot even-par 70 on Sunday to win the 1999 U.S. Open. Stewart's was a different kind of great round. It wasn't about shooting a low score, because only two players broke par on that Sunday. Winning the U.S. Open is about survival and making pars. It's not a birdie-fest. Stewart's round required a different mind-set, one of patience, emotional control, and guts.

It takes a special mind-set to shoot low and break personal scoring barriers at any level of golf. A player can't let expectations of what a good score is affect his or her ability to play well. Let's look at a few players who used superior mind power to play their way into record books.

The Go-Low Mentality

What do Ernie Els, Tiger Woods, Laura Davies, and John Huston all have in common? Besides being great players, they all go low often. John Huston, for example, set a new 72-hole PGA Tour scoring record at the 1999 Hawaiian Open with a score of 28 under par. Do these players possess unusual abilities that help them shoot lights out? Obviously, they are all very talented players with tons of physical ability and they have honed their skills diligently over their careers—but talent and practice can take them only so far. Chip Beck said it best: "Part of greatness is having a natural gift, but part of it is development of that gift. So it's a real blending of the two. If you take someone like Greg Norman, who is really gifted and who has really developed his talent, he has won a lot of tournaments. I don't think he would have done as well with an attitude of comme ci, comme ca [*sic*]."

> *Thoughts of doing something exciting in the game, more extraordinary than the average—that's part of what makes people peak perform.*
>
> —CHIP BECK

These great players have attributes other than physical talent that help them shoot low scores. They have a strong motivation toward low scoring. Great players know they can conquer any course they play. When they get in the zone, confidence and momentum kick in. But they don't let distractions pull them off task. They don't get carried away by the excitement of going low. They stay focused in the present—on the one shot they are playing. And when they get it going, there is no backing off; they know how to run the tables. Comfort zones do not confine them. Expectations about what a good score is don't restrict them. Doubts about reversing ground with a bogey don't enter their minds. Challenging shots don't make them back down. Once in the zone, they go with the flow and ride momentum to the end of the round or tournament.

Breaking Through Your Own Barriers

Going Low is about breaking mental and scoring barriers. You, like other golfers, expect to shoot a certain score every time you play. Professional golfers expect to shoot par or better every day they play. Some have higher standards, such as Ernie Els, whose goal is to shoot 68 every day. You, too, have a "comfort zone" or scoring zone that reflects what you think you can shoot every time you play. If you're a 15-handicap, for example, you expect to shoot between 84 and 90 on most days. You expect to shoot scores that match your perceived skill level and past level of play.

If you are an amateur trying to break 90 for the first time, you are playing a different game from the one a pro plays. You can make two or three double bogeys, several bogeys, plus a couple of pars and still break 90. Bogey golf is the standard of par for the golfer trying to break 90 for the first time. This means hitting greens in one shot over regulation (i.e., hitting a par 4 in three) and two-putting each hole for bogey. You and I both know it's not that simple. For a 20-handicap, keeping the ball in play or two-putting from 40 feet is a challenge, not to mention the two balls hit in the water and the ball that was sliced out of bounds. This player may hit two to four greens in regulation and have a couple of chances at birdie. It's not as consistent as David Duval's round of 59, where he hit 17 greens in regulation, but for the 20-handicap, it feels consistent and it gets the job done.

Even though you don't play as consistently as David Duval, you can still learn a great deal from him and from other pros who have shot their lowest rounds. To shoot a 59, David Duval must do more than hit good shots and make putts. He must be in a focused state of mind, feel confident in his skills, and play the course smartly. I emphasize state of mind here. He must be keenly focused in the present moment, not be afraid to make mistakes, quickly brush off distractions, deal with the antics of his playing partners, and cope with the emotions and excitement of shooting a career-low 59—all while trying to win a golf tournament. To achieve this, he would naturally need to prepare his mind for the round, play strategic golf, and have the discipline, focus, and patience to keep a good round going. All these traits are just as important for you when the time comes for you to play your best. You will learn all about them in this book.

I first got the idea for writing *Going Low* after talking to several players who had recently recorded their career-low rounds. From my discussions with these players, I found that they described the experience of taking it deep similarly, which identified a certain mind-set for going low. My goal is to share this information with you. I've worked with players of all levels on the mental game of golf for over 12 years. The vast majority of my work is with professionals, but I have also worked extensively with amateurs of all levels, including juniors, high-handicap golfers, and college golfers. Yes, pros do play a different game than amateurs, but I believe that you can learn great and useful lessons in these pages about how pros manage their games, both mentally and strategically.

What is a great round for a tour pro? Depending on the course and the weather conditions, a great round produces a score in the low to mid-60s. To shoot in the 60s, a player must hit 15 to 16 greens in regulation. Most pros play well from tee to green, or they wouldn't be playing professionally. The difference between a 72 and a 68 is having four putts lip out instead of fall in. A great round for you may be to break 90 or 80 or 70 for the first time. In *Going Low* you will learn how to harness your emotions and focus properly to play your best round ever and continue to break barriers.

What prevents amateurs from shooting the scores they are capable of? I believe many players limit themselves with so-called comfort zones, just to mention one barrier. A comfort zone becomes a problem whenever a player is playing better than expected or is breaking new ground. In this book, I teach you how to break out of self-limiting expectations and preconceived beliefs. Comfort zones don't limit great players on tour, such as David Duval, Tiger Woods, and Davis Love III. Comfort zones actually benefit pro golfers when they can bring a poor round back into their scoring zone and turn a score of 76 into a 72. When going low, they don't just try to "get it in the clubhouse" when they get to four under par after 12 holes. If a pro gets to four under par after 12, that's great, but he doesn't stop there. His goal is to get to five under. This attitude, adopted by many professionals, is far from the mind-set of the amateur who is playing better than expected or on the verge of shooting a personal-best score.

Many golfers often ask me the same question: "What's the one thing you can tell me about the mental game of golf that can help me play better?" This is a tough question to answer, for the simple reason that every golfer is different. Each golfer has a different personality, background, skill level, and mental makeup. Obviously, confidence is important for every golfer, but how each player develops and loses confidence may be totally different. This is the difficulty of writing a book on the mental game of golf. The challenge is to write a book that applies to a wide range of playing abilities, personalities, and belief systems.

What I do know from working with golfers at all levels is that good players possess the same "basic" mental skills, just as they possess the basics of a good golf swing. No two golfers have the same swing, and no two golfers have the same mental makeup. Part of performing well every day requires what I call the Three C's—confidence, concentration, and composure. You probably throw around these words often in golf and at work because they are so important to success, but do you really know how to develop and harness the Three C's?

I talk a lot about self-confidence in my work because it's the most critical psychological attribute for success. Confidence is how strongly you believe in your ability to perform. Confidence is derived from a baseline of past play, practice, and preparation. A beginning golfer has little to no confidence in his ability to make a 30-foot putt. With practice, he becomes competent in the basic putting skills. *With competency or skill mastery comes confidence.* There are a couple of exceptions. A golfer can bring confidence to golf from other sports or activities in which he has been successful, or he can simply derive his confidence from the belief that he is physically talented. Later in the book, you will learn about how to harness the power of confidence before the round starts so you can get off to a strong start and capture momentum.

The second C, concentration or focus, is also very important to your success. Think of concentration not as feverish mental intensity but as a requirement that you pay attention to detail in the present moment. Without a here-and-now focus on the requirements of the task, the mind is free to wander to things unrelated to your immediate performance. It's been called playing one shot at a time or staying focused on the task. Players talk about this concept often, but not too many really know how to achieve it. Concentration is particularly important for the golfer who wants to shoot a personal-best round but is hindered by distractions or internal mind games.

The third C, composure or emotional control, is important for golfers who get too excited, frustrated, or upset on the golf course. It's rare to find a golfer who is totally composed and calm in the throes of adversity. Occasionally, I'll meet this type of golfer, but not often. Many perfectionistic, goal-driven golfers need help with composure. The more you "invest" in golf and the more driven you are to achieve, the easier it is to become frustrated and upset when you don't play up to expectations. Then, on the day when your expectations are finally achieved, you may have to fight off disbelief and the sense of what-do-I-do-now? Playing well is exciting—for some, too exciting. This is when the skill of composure must go to work.

Although the Three C's are very important to playing your best golf every day, going low involves more than that. Shooting a personal-best round requires that you identify and eliminate self-limiting, preconceived beliefs and behaviors. For example, how often have you been in the middle of playing a good round and said to yourself: "When am I going to screw up a hole and make my first double bogey?" only to do just that on the next hole? In everything you do in life, your beliefs shape your perceptions and thus guide your behavior. You will learn in this book how to shed self-limiting beliefs so you can open your mind to great possibilities.

Shooting a personal-best round requires other important skills. Great golfers play well because they know how to practice efficiently, are dedicated to improvement, and know the best way to prepare themselves for a round of great golf. I'm not talking about hitting two buckets of balls to get ready for tomorrow's match. Pros are dedicated to quality practice, focused preparation, and improving their games daily. This is the foundation for the development of confidence.

To shoot a personal-low round you need to know how to prepare to play the course, set a strategic game plan, and deal with the distractions of the group. You also need to practice in a way that makes your swing repeatable. You must learn how to score your best when it counts, and simplify your game so you can focus on playing golf instead of always working and grinding at it. In *Going Low*, you'll learn how to accomplish each of these requirements so you can put it all together and go low. Here are the specific lessons you will learn:

Chapter 1 describes how you can unlock the self-imposed limits of your own success. I'll teach you how to first identify your own mental barriers and reveal to you the unhealthy beliefs that prevent you from consistently playing your best. Then I'll show you how to eradicate unhealthy expectations and irrational beliefs so you can unlock the self-imposed limits of your own success. To help do this, we'll examine sporting records that were once thought to be unbreakable, such as the four-minute mile, but were broken repeatedly.

Chapter 2 teaches the second important lesson in going low: how to be confident before you even hit a shot, develop momentum early in a round, and spark momentum when it's slow to start. If you want to play well right out of the gate, you must learn how to harness confidence and capture early momentum. By studying the best players in the world, you will understand how to be confident and create momentum right from the start.

Chapter 3 discusses an important factor in low scoring—the ability to play with feel, imagination, and cleverness, not mechanical perfection. Scoring is the name of the game, not making pretty swings and hitting perfect shots on the practice range. You will learn how to transcend the mechanics of the game by playing freely and letting it happen. To do this you first need to understand the difference between learning and performance. You will learn how to practice to make your swing repeatable and how to play golf unencumbered by mechanical thoughts.

Chapter 4 teaches you two lessons central to playing good golf: how to adopt a simplistic approach to golf and how to play within your abilities. Both lessons are discussed in the context of going low. You'll learn how to simplify golf by not overthinking, by eliminating judgmental thinking, and by finding techniques to calm the mind. Playing what may feel like ho-hum golf, and not trying too hard to shoot a low score, is what it takes to play your best.

Chapter 5 shows you how to identify and effectively cope with mental traps during a low round, such as social evaluation (what others may be thinking of you), self-consciousness, stage fright (being the center of attention), and negative group dynamics. Many golfers invent ways to foul up a good round. I'll show you how to deal with the inner turmoil and challenges of breaking new ground and how the dynamics of the group (player personalities, psychouts, betting, etc.) can influence your final score.

Chapter 6 teaches the central lesson of how golfers can overcome the negative effect of comfort zones, which I introduce in Chapter 1. To carry a good round to the end, you need to keep a "task focus," use good course management, and push yourself to stay aggressive and not play protective. This includes learning—on each successive low round you shoot—how to do all these better. You will learn how pros eliminate comfort zones and how to break your personal scoring barrier.

Chapter 7 teaches you how to keep golf in perspective and take a balanced approach to life and golf. The focus of this chapter is keeping your priorities straight, maintaining healthy expectations for your golf game, and understanding golf's place in your life. Golf can at times take over your life and dominate the feelings you carry with you every day. You will learn how to balance the importance of golf with other activities. I'll give you examples of pros who have shot their lowest rounds by keeping golf in perspective.

Chapter 8 is a lesson in how to post more low rounds by lowering your "scoring zone" after making a breakthrough. Here I teach you how to accept low scores, reward yourself for shooting low scores, and believe low scores are the norm and not the exception so you can continue to shoot low rounds. You will learn how to follow a breakthrough round with more low rounds and keep on making more breakthroughs. You'll learn how to commit to getting better and improving your skills every day by setting appropriate goals, monitoring your progress, and modifying goals to continue to break new ground.

Chapter 9 teaches you specific lessons for breaking the 100, 90, 80, and 70 milestones. Specific methods for both high-handicap and low-handicap players are given to help both classes of golfers make more scoring breakthroughs. By reading examples of how a player makes a breakthrough, you will learn how to shoot your best score ever.

The Appendix provides solutions to the most common problems that comfort zones and mental barriers present. I give you answers to real questions that you would ask me if you had the opportunity. I answer questions that golfers should ask but haven't, as well as questions from actual golfers who want solutions to their specific golfing dilemmas.

All of the lessons in *Going Low* build upon one another. Low scoring starts when you can eradicate preconceived beliefs that limit your success in golf and maybe other endeavors, as well. With your mind opened up to the possibilities, you are receptive to playing your best golf. Then I take you through the round from the start to the finish and thereafter. To harness momentum, you need to prepare to be confident and get in the right mind-set for the start of the round. A great start boosts confidence, but playing well (or too well) can make some golfers nervous about not screwing up a good round. The rest of the book teaches you "how to get over the hump" by giving you the know-how to turn a good-round-in-the-making into a personal-best round. Then, finally, you will learn how to continue to break new ground after shooting a recent personal-best round. It's perfectly fine to relish your success for a while, but you can't let satisfaction or complacency sap your motivation to strive for even greater success.

Before you can cover 18 holes in a breakthrough low score, you must first take a complete tour of your inner thoughts and emotions. We'll start that tour by examining how different your approach to shooting a low round is compared to those golfers who shoot the lowest scores ever recorded.

Breaking Free of
Mental Barriers

There are no limits to what you can do, except for your own.
—SCOTT VERPLANK (CAREER LOW: 62)

Jack Nicklaus won an astonishing 20 majors in his career. Babe Didrikson Zaharias won a staggering 27 tournament titles in 1947. Byron Nelson won an implausible 11 titles in a row in 1945 and finished with 18 wins that season. Sam Snead won a record 81 career PGA Tour victories. These well-known and long-standing records may never be broken. With so much depth of talent on the professional tours today, it will be very difficult to break records such as Byron Nelson's 11 titles in a row.

Obviously, athletes (including golfers) don't set records or shatter them unless they possess tremendous skill. But even more central to surpassing past records are a player's self-defined limitations about what he or she thinks is possible to achieve. Humans have much greater resources for success than they tend to use. Scientists say that we use only 10 to 15 percent of our brain's capacity, for example. Golfers are similar in that they often stifle their own success with self-imposed psychological limits.

Self-limiting behavior comes in many forms. It includes preconceived notions, unhealthy expectations, and irrational thoughts you may have formed about your abilities, skills, and chances of success. The sum of your experiences over a lifetime—your upbringing, your education, and your interaction with others—have shaped your beliefs and expectations. Some of these beliefs are rational and helpful, and others are irrational and harmful. The purpose of this chapter is to teach you how to identify and eradicate the beliefs that impede your success in golf, as well as in other endeavors in your life.

If you examine the psychological makeup of history's greatest athletes, the ones who have broken long-standing records, you'll see that a pattern exists among them. These athletes had the ability to rise above their own expectations and break records that were considered beyond reach. It's clear that these people were not conformers; they were not confined by the expectations of others. Somehow, the great record-breaking athletes buffered themselves against the negative (constrictive) expectations of others. They were open-minded to the idea of breaking records that most people considered out of reach.

Sporting records that have stood the test of time represent the highest achievement of human potential and thus become both mental and physical obstacles for athletes to break through. Once an athlete overcomes a mental or physical barrier, suddenly the barrier no longer exists and new expectations or limits of what is possible are formed.

Perhaps the classic case of this is Roger Bannister, the first person to run the mile in less than four minutes. Before Bannister broke the mile barrier, scientists believed that it was physically impossible for a human to cover that amount of ground in less than four minutes because the previous record time of 4:01.3 had stood for nine years. Bannister broke the four-minute-mile barrier in 1954 with a time of 3:59.4. That changed everyone's thinking about the mile run. Within four years of Bannister's run, 16 other runners had broken the barrier. In hindsight, Bannister's time seems more impressive because he ran it in a 15-mile-per-hour crosswind with gusts that reached 25 mph. It took a decade for the next "untouchable" barrier to be broken when New Zealand's John Walker ran the mile in 3:49.4. When asked to explain his record run, Bannister said, "It's the ability to take more out of yourself than you've got." This is a crucial point that we will certainly revisit.

Another record-breaking feat that awed the sports world was Bob Beamon's long jump at the 1968 Olympics. Beamon made a leap of 29'2½", setting a record that would stand for 23 years. What's amazing about his jump is that no one had ever before jumped even 28 feet. In the same jump, Beamon became the first long jumper to clear the 28-foot and 29-foot barriers! In fact, the next 28-foot-long jump did not occur until the 1980 Olympics, 12 years later, when Lutz Dombrowski did it. Beamon's astounding jump increased the world record by 21¾ inches.

Mark McGwire is a modern-day example of an athlete who doesn't cower in the face of legendary records. During the 1998 baseball season, McGwire and his rival, Sammy Sosa, both chased Roger Maris's 37-year-old single-season home-run record. Before Roger Maris hit 61 homers in a single season, Babe Ruth's record of 60 homers had stood for 34 years. In 1998, 27 years after Maris's 61 homers, Mark McGwire shattered the record with 70 homers in a season. "I think it will stand for a while. I know how grueling it is to do what I've done this year," McGwire said. McGwire and Sosa battled it out the entire season, with McGwire holding the lead most of the way. Sosa led briefly just twice during the season—when he hit his 48th and 49th homers in the same game at Chicago, and again, later in the season, when he hit his 66th before McGwire countered with two homers of his own. I have to believe that the competition between Sosa and McGwire helped both players push beyond mental obstacles and plow through preconceptions of what they could achieve in the season.

These examples from other sports highlight the importance of putting aside preconceptions of what is possible to achieve, to not inherit the expectations of others in society, and to rise above one's own doubts in order to break through mental hurdles before breaking through physical ones.

Self-Imposed Roadblocks to Success

These examples lead to a central question: why do people, golfers included, place psychological limits on their own success? There are many reasons, but isn't it strange how these reasons all disappear when a barrier does finally break down? At that point, an opposite belief takes over, a belief that, if a feat can be accomplished once, it can be accomplished over and over again. When great people break records or successfully navigate unknown waters, it changes everyone's thinking. I'm sure you can think of many other examples in history when this has happened.

How does all this apply to your golf game? It's probable that you, like many other golfers, are confined to a belief system that says "it's not possible because I haven't proven it's possible—by doing it." This negative definition will always hold you back from playing to your potential. Until you completely convince yourself that a certain achievement is readily possible, that achievement is beyond your reach. Simply put, if you don't think you can do it, how will you be able to succeed? Breaking 60 in professional golf was always thought to be an impossible barrier until Al Geiberger shot his 59 in 1997. To date, four other golfers have achieved that score in competition. One of them, Notah Begay, who shot 59 in competition, believes he can shoot a 58 or 57 during his career, which is the first step in making it become a reality. I strongly advise you to follow his cue. If you have never broken 90 or 80 or 70, whichever score is your personal barrier, that number becomes a mental hurdle or a personal "record" for you to break. You can do so only by mentally defining this achievement as a valid possibility.

Take the example of a golfer named Trevor. His lowest score is 82, and he tells me he usually shoots between 84 and 92 depending on the course, but he expects to shoot 85 if he plays well. He also says if he plays well on the front and shoots 39, he usually shoots 45 or higher on the back. It's hard for him to keep that good round going. But when he plays poorly on the front and shoots a 49, he can usually bring it back to a respectable score and shoot 41 on the back. What is Trevor's limiting belief? Based on his past experience, he believes that every day he plays he will shoot between 84 and 92, which becomes a self-fulfilling prophecy. Trevor allows other counterproductive thoughts into his head during the round, such as "I always find a way to mess up a good round on the back nine after playing well on the front side." Ever said these words yourself?

Trevor's preconceptions and expectations about his ability to score form his personal comfort zone. If he gets off to a great start to the round—say, one under after three holes—this score doesn't match his expected scoring ability. Consequently, he sabotages his own game with negative thoughts such as "When am I going to make my first double bogey and screw this up?" It's the same process at work when he shoots 40 on the front nine. That score doesn't match his belief system, so it triggers thoughts of past rounds, in which he indeed found a way to foul things up. His thought "I always manage to mess up when I have a good round going" is irrational and based on a generalization. It is irrational primarily because it prevents him from achieving his purpose and desire, which is to shoot the score his front-nine play has positioned him for.

There is a positive side to this way of thinking, however: generalizations can also work in one's favor. In the past, when Trevor shot a poor front nine, he has been able to play pretty well on the back nine. The thought "I'm a better player than my score indicates on the front" allows him to have the confidence that he can play better on the back. Essentially, he is able to shoot himself back into his comfort zone. A comfort zone, which worked against him when he played better than expected, also worked for him when he played worse than expected. Is this rational? It's definitely more sensible. It's more sensible because Trevor uses his past experience to make himself believe he can play better on the back.

What's Trevor's psychological barrier? His best score is 82, so shooting 81 or 80 would be very satisfying to him. But once a player like Trevor proves to himself he is capable of shooting scores in the low 80s, a 79 seems very enticing and thus becomes the elusive goal. Any golfer who can shoot in the 80s, for example, would love to be a 70s shooter. Likewise, a golfer who shoots in the 100s would love to break into the 90s. It's a mental breakthrough for the golfer. In Trevor's case, if he breaks into the 70s, he now feels ready to shoot more scores in the 70s. But how can he shoot 79 when his lowest score is 82 with what he thought was a lucky round? On most days, the reality is that he shoots 84 or higher. If you fall into the same trap as Trevor, the first task is to identify self-limiting beliefs, irrational thoughts, and constrictive expectations that hold you back from taking it deep.

Breaking Free of Restrictive Beliefs

Identifying the problem behavior is the first step to changing any behavior. In this case, you need to identify beliefs or preconceptions that become negative self-fulfilling prophecies that limit your golfing success. I'll give you a head start by identifying the most commonly seen irrational and self-limiting beliefs and show how each one operates. I'll also give you the remedy to each limiting belief. The focus here is on beliefs that are self-destructive to shooting your best round ever. Here are seven prime examples:

Syndrome 1: "I'll most likely shoot . . ."

A prediction of this type is the root of comfort zones. It's the most common self-destructive belief among golfers, and Trevor, as you could see, is a perfect example of it. This expectation-based syndrome is rooted in what you think is a realistic score for the day. How can you ever lower your scoring zone if you think that you will always score within an expected range? Your only possible chance to play above your expectations is to get lucky one day. You are what you think you are. In this case, you can shoot only what you think is possible to shoot.

Remedy 1: Throw Away Target Scores

The first step in breaking free of preconceptions is to not set target scores or focus on what score you want to shoot any given day. Target scores are nothing more than expectations in disguise. If you're a 20-handicap and you are happy with "bogey golf," you'll play for a bogey on every hole. With this attitude, you will most likely fall short and make too many double bogeys. The same is true for golf-ers on the pro tours who focus too much on making "the cut" so they can play on the weekend. Adopting an attitude of "I need to make the cut," they end up focusing too much on the cut, ride the cut line, and either make or miss it by a shot. This is why Tiger Woods's goal is to win every tournament he plays. Yes, he has a ton of confidence and it's a lot to ask of himself, but he sets his sights high to push himself toward excellence. If he falls short of winning, he earns a top 10.

Most golfers who play the Tour avoid setting target scores. Scott Verplank is one example of a player who achieved a career-low round using this philosophy, shooting 62 one year in the Milwaukee Open. He believes golfers should not make judgments before they play about what is a good score to shoot. Verplank said: "You limit your game by paying attention to your environment, what other people think is a good score, and what you think is a good score." He plays his best golf, as do many golfers, when he doesn't focus on score. "If you don't think about score and you just play the game and prepare yourself before you tee it up, there is no limit to what you can shoot. If you don't pay attention to score, then your ability to shoot low is increased," Verplank said.

For me, if you are oblivious to the score, then you usually play pretty well."

—BILLY MAYFAIR

Billy Mayfair is another example of a player who doesn't pay attention to score. In 1993, Billy shot a career-low 61 in the second round of the GTE Byron Nelson Classic. He considers himself a consistent player who scores in the low 70s to upper 60s, but he doesn't go low as often as some other players on tour. He is simi-lar to many other tour pros in that he gets immersed in playing the game and thus loses sight of score. Mayfair said this about his career-low round: "You have to keep a cap on your emotions, but when you get it going that low, you just have to try to have fun. And to be honest with you, I really lost track of how many under

I was, and I didn't know it was for a course record, either, until after I was done."

Syndrome 2: "Here I go again."

This is a generalization made about your own game based on experience. Have you ever said to yourself, "Here I go again, playing like an idiot"? If so, you are a prisoner of this syndrome. This thinking process becomes a self-fulfilling prophecy that influences your behavior on the golf course. If you think you are playing "like an idiot," you will probably find a way to play it out. Players engage in several forms of "here I go again":

"Here I go again—messing up another good round with a double bogey."
"Here I go again—making a stupid high number, which negates my entire round."
"Here I go again—following a great first nine with bogus play on the back."
"Here I go again—finding a way to shoot myself in the foot the last three holes."
"Here I go again—blowing the lead I had early in the match."

Remedy 2: It's a New Day, New Game

I've often worked with players who think that a poor start to a round is a bad omen for the rest of the round. I strongly discourage this kind of thinking. Just because it's happened before doesn't mean history will repeat itself. Some people take generalizations to an extreme. I worked with a college golfer who had to fold his glove a certain way in order to have his best chance at making birdie on the next hole. The power of a self-fulfilling prophecy makes you truly believe that if something happened in the past it will happen again. Every day is different. Every game is different. How many rounds have you played in which you finished well after a poor start? Do you ever remember those rounds when you get off to a poor start? It's irrational to generalize that history will repeat itself in the negative but not the positive.

Syndrome 3: "I'll never do it."

If you are a pessimist or a negative thinker, you believe that you will never break 90 no matter how hard you try. Every mistake, double bogey, or bit of bad luck is perceived as a sign that you won't shoot a low score. You judge yourself harshly by adopting negative labels to describe your game, such as "worst putter in the world" or "banana ball man." By internalizing negative labels, you live them out during play.

Remedy 3: Use Positive Labels

Your problem is that you maintain too many negative labels. To be your own best friend, you need to use positive terms to describe yourself. First, you have to discard your negative labels, such as "worst putter in the world." How will you ever make putts or be a good putter with this type of thinking? It becomes part of your self-concept. Replace your negative labels with more "golfer-friendly" labels. Also, don't adopt negative labels that others give you, such as when someone says, "Gee, you can't buy a putt today."

Syndrome 4: "I'm not that good."

This is a form of self-destructive denial in which the player downplays her success. If this is you, the culprit is your negative self-image. You always invalidate the good rounds you've played by believing that you are not as good as the results indicated. A player stuck in the "I'm not that good" syndrome has a hard time developing confidence. She will always find a reason to disqualify her positive experiences because of a lack of confidence and a poor self-image.

Remedy 4: Become More Self-Rewarding

If you always disqualify your successes, even small ones, you will find it hard to develop confidence. Even some confident tour pros fall into this trap. When their standards become excessively high, they think they are supposed to hit great shots and make all their putts. For them, hitting a great shot is no longer satisfying. For you, a poor self-image is the culprit. "It was just a lucky shot," you say. You just can't believe you are good enough to hit a great shot or sink a long putt—it doesn't match your golfing self-image. You need to change your thinking. First, reward yourself for good shots and putts or for shooting a good round. Second, learn to accept compliments from others and integrate them into your identity. Third, see failure or errors as learning experiences, a way to improve.

Johnny Miller's 63: An Out-of-Body Experience

Before the final round of the 1973 U.S. Open, Johnny Miller was struggling on the range with his swing. On the first tee, a thought popped into his head: "Open your stance way up." He listened, and his body obeyed. His closing 63 at Oakmont Country Club is considered one of the best low-scoring rounds in history. His round was an against-all-odds story. He had to contend with the pressure of a final round in the U.S. Open, chase leader and favorite Arnold Palmer, come from six shots back, and play on what many people regard as the most difficult course in the United States.

Miller recalls his final-round 63 as an out-of-body experience. Just how good was his 63? Only two other players broke 70 that afternoon: Jack Nicklaus (68) and Lanny Wadkins (65). Miller claims it was the best round, tee to green, he ever had. After making birdie on the first four holes, Miller felt he was making ground on the leaders and thus letting them know he was in contention. After a par on the fifth, he made a three-putt bogey at the tough eighth hole, but he birdied the ninth to shoot 32 on the front. He felt a strange calmness come over him after the eighth hole, almost as though it wasn't he playing. He felt it was his day to win. After making par on 10, Miller made three birdies in a row at 11, 12, 13, and then another at 15. He was now eight under for the day and felt right then he had won the Open. He two-putted for par at the 16th and 17th holes and missed a 15-footer for birdie on 18.

His 63 is the lowest final round in Open history—not just the lowest by an Open winner. "I feel like of all the rounds I ever played, that one was touched by someone upstairs," Miller said. "I struggled to get my game, then one inspirational tip and I hit the ball like a machine. It was like it was meant to be."

Syndrome 5: "I can't make mistakes."

Most perfectionists are trapped in this syndrome. If you think this way, one mistake makes you believe that the whole round is wasted—"a perfect round ruined again." As the round progresses, the tension builds as you try to avoid that one "fatal" mistake. If a round goes south, it's easy for you to become frustrated. This leads to trying harder or giving up on the round altogether. Another characteristic of this syndrome is analyzing your round by how many mistakes you made and tallying what you would have scored without making those mistakes.

Remedy 5: Be More Accepting

Perfectionists have a very hard time accepting their mistakes. The goal is a flawless round, and when this doesn't happen, perfectionists become critical, judgmental, and pessimistic. I've done more than a hundred interviews with golfers on the subject of peak performance, and I can assure you the professionals do not fall into this trap. Not one successful pro player believes a perfect round is possible. You will always make one or two mistakes, even when playing your best. First, forget about playing a perfect, mistake-free round. Second, give yourself the opportunity to make three or four mistakes during the round. That way you can play on with composure when you make a mistake. Third, when you do make a mistake or hit an "unacceptable" shot, view it as part of golf and know that you can recover if you maintain your composure.

Syndrome 6: "I don't have it today."

This negative belief causes many golfers to presuppose that every phase of the game must be in top shape to shoot a low round. This is a form of overgeneralization. If you engage in this type of thinking and any one part of your game is not up to standard, then you will believe it's impossible to shoot a good round. Even though you have scored well when playing less than perfectly in the past, you have formed a destructive belief. This false conclusion is based on the idea that a great round can result only from great ball-striking and flawless putting. When you have this mind-set and you start to play poorly, it's easy to give up on the round.

Remedy 6: Grind It Out and Scramble

Professional golfers don't pack their bags in the middle of the second round before the two-day cut if they think they may be out of the tournament. They continue to grind out the round. Their mindset is to get the ball in the hole and not worry about how they are hitting it. The possibility always exists that they can make a great comeback down the stretch. The thought "I don't have it today" becomes another self-fulfilling prophecy. So instead of worrying about a part of your game that is not up to par, focus on your strengths. Great putting can make up for a lot of missed shots. And good course management can help you to keep the round together when you are not on top of your game, a subject that I will discuss in Chapter 9.

Syndrome 7: "I am only as good as my last score."

This last syndrome is a self-defeating belief that is rooted in one's self-esteem. If you get upset after a bad round and it makes you feel mildly depressed the rest of the day, then you are a victim of this syndrome. You have low self-esteem if you can feel happy about yourself only when you play well. The problem is that you tie golf to your self-esteem. You desperately want to prove yourself to others to gain their respect via golf. Thus, you pay more attention to what playing partners may be thinking about you than playing golf. You also try too hard to play well because your ego is riding on how well you play.

Remedy 7: Realize You Are "More Than a Score"

In today's society, we are taught that success is the route to personal self-worth. We are bombarded by images in the media, on television, and at work that make us believe we can only feel worthy if we are successful, which is false. Many golfers buy into this irrational belief. You need to distinguish who you are from your golf game, and the first step is to learn how to separate your performance in golf from your self-worth. Let's put golf in perspective with your life. Golf is just one activity in your life; it doesn't define who you are. And that last round you played is only one day of your golfing pursuits.

Challenge Your Own Thinking

Humans are born with the capacity to behave both rationally and irrationally. I would like you to try to identify irrational beliefs that restrict you from playing up to personal par today. How do people know when they are harboring restrictive beliefs? First, ask yourself an important question: "Are my beliefs in line with what I want to achieve?" If your answer is yes, you are on your way to playing uninhibited golf. If you entertain beliefs such as "I never play up to my potential," you are in need of exorcising beliefs that prevent you from playing up to your potential. Your beliefs and expectations color the way you perceive the world and interact with your environment. Any mistakes, mishaps, and bad luck will be interpreted as signals that reinforce your defeatist belief.

Challenging your own thinking process means you are testing to see if the underlying belief is self-defeating or self-empowering. The first test is to ask yourself if a belief such as "I never play up to my potential" serves you well. Most likely, it doesn't. The next step is to challenge the reality of the belief by asking another question: "What proof supports my conclusion?" In other words, what has happened in the past that makes you think you never play up to your potential? "Did I truly come to a logical conclusion?" If you can only conclude that this statement is true, then does it mean the pattern must continue? Disputing your own belief system is a very direct way of identifying and uprooting unhealthy beliefs that limit your success.

Change Your Lingo

Have your ever entered into a money match with your buddies and asked yourself, "What if I fail and embarrass myself?" If you are guilty of this, what does it say about your mind-set? The terminology used to describe this situation says a lot about your motive. In this case, it says that you are motivated to avoid failure. On the course, your primary goal is to not mess up, blow a lead, lose money, and/or make a fool out of yourself. This is not a healthy approach to playing golf.

One method used to change your mind-set is to change your own lingo. The goal is to abolish negative, defeatist statements and use more positive, productive statements. You do have a choice in this matter. You have control over your self-talk. Here are a few examples of defeatist self-statements and a corresponding productive self-statement for each:

Defeatist Self-Talk	Productive Self-Talk
Great front nine; don't blow it on the back.	Keep this round going strong.
Play it safe so you don't blow the lead.	Play your game and bury him.
Don't hook it left and make a double bogey.	Pick a smart target on the right side.

He's got me again; I always lose to this guy.	Two holes left—I can recover.
I'm never going to break 90.	I can't wait until I break 90.

In addition, it's also helpful to eliminate absolute thinking, because this is very closely tied to expectations. People who think in absolutes have high demands and no tolerance for poor performance. They use constricting terms such as "must," "have to," "need to," and "should" to describe their disposition. For example, do you believe that you need to hit the ball well to play your best? Absolute thinking limits your ability to be flexible and adapt to any situation, especially when you are not playing as well as expected.

Absolute Thinking	**Flexible Thinking**
I need to hit the ball well to score well.	I prefer to hit it well to score well.
I should never make a double bogey.	Doubles aren't fun, but I can recover.
I have to win this match today.	I believe I can win this match today.
I must shoot better on the back nine.	I know I can play better on the back nine.

Final Thoughts

This is probably as much a motivational chapter as an instructional chapter. The main question I pose is How can you ever break a personal scoring record when your belief system hinders achievement? To make a scoring breakthrough, you will need to do more than buy a new putter, change golf clubs, buy a different golf ball, or take more golf lessons. You might get lucky and shoot a low round one day. Another, more preferable option is to use an erasable pencil to mark scores on the scorecard, but that doesn't cut it either.

I think golfers get overconcerned with results. Enjoy the process; enjoy the opportunity to play.
— WENDY WARD

A better option is to discard self-defeating beliefs, self-limiting expectations, and negative self-talk that hold you back from playing your best. First, you must be willing to look inside and identify self-destructive philosophies and replace them with more logical, self-enhancing beliefs. Second, you must learn to play golf without imposing any expectations about what you should score, how well you should hit the ball, or how many putts you should make. Finally, you have to develop healthy beliefs grounded in principles that allow you to strive for greatness.

TWO

Getting, Keeping, and Controlling Momentum

Once I get going, I tend to keep it going. And maybe that's just because how emotional I am when I play; I get fired up and I enjoy it.

—TIGER WOODS (CAREER LOW: 61)

As I walk confidently onto the range to hit a few warm-up balls before the Club Championship at The Meadows Country Club, I wonder with whom I am paired today. Grabbing a few clubs to take to the range, I see several players, many of whom I know well, warming up before the first round. I've played golf several times with many members of the club, and I pretty much know each player's game and how they approach tournaments. I also know which golfers will play well right from the first tee and which players will struggle early in the round.

The first player I notice is John, because he just hit a big hook with his driver. Whoops! I know a poor warm-up doesn't bother John the least bit. John is a competitive player. He'll play well today, because he won't let bad shots on the range ruin his confidence for the opening holes. John's not big on practice—in fact, he hates to practice—but when he gets on the course, he is like a man possessed. He is always more focused on the course than on the range. I think it's his love of competition and belief in his ability that helps him focus and play well. He believes he can beat anyone he plays against, even though he doesn't practice much. I wonder how good John could be if he practiced more. I like playing with John because he is all business when it's his turn to play, but he loves to talk and relax on the golf course. He'll play solid at the start of the round because he seems to "will" the ball into the hole and he thrives on tournament play.

Randy is beside John, beating balls. Randy is a streaky golfer. Off the course, Randy is a friend of mine. On the course, he can turn into a hothead if he doesn't play well, and that's why I don't want to be paired with him, especially if he plays poorly. I can tell when he is mentally shot for the day, because when he gets off to a bad start, he talks himself into shooting in the low 90s. He hates making a big number on the first few holes, because he always expects to par or birdie the first holes—especially when he hits the ball well in warm-up. Randy can play good golf on occasion, in the low 80s, but only when he starts the round with a couple of solid holes and feels some confidence. That early confidence and momentum carry him for the rest of the round. Instead of the usual temper tantrums and ominous predictions about his score after he starts poorly, Randy focuses on playing each hole and each shot to the best of his ability. I like playing with Randy when he plays well, but you don't want to be near him when he plays poorly.

The next player I see is Rick, who is talking to Joe instead of getting ready to play. Rick is a social golfer. Rick really isn't into golf like John. He has told me that he likes the social part of golf more than the competition. He'll shoot a good score from time to time, but he isn't interested in winning or beating others, as John is. He never gets nervous or upset on the golf course, because to him golf is played for fun and relaxation. And he doesn't work on his game and try to get better. He prefers to play well, but playing bad golf does not change his attitude. A bad or good start to the round won't affect him one way or the other, so he plays consistent golf from one round to the next. He's fun and relaxed on the course, but I know he's not interested in a side bet, so it's a wash if I play with him today.

As I begin to stretch before hitting balls, I can see that Joe is getting irritated with Rick. Joe just wants to focus on getting a good warm-up before he plays. Joe plays self-conscious golf. Joe doesn't want Rick to think he's a jerk by cutting the conversation short. He worries too much about how others perceive him as a person and as a golfer. His main goal is to earn the respect from others via his golf game, thus making golf a test of his own self-worth. He gets so nervous sometimes that he has to run to the bathroom just after he tees his ball up on the first hole. Joe always gets off to a rough start and needs three or four holes just to settle down, compose himself, and play his game. When he does settle down he plays OK, but he still worries too much about what others think about his swing, game, and him as a person during the round. He dearly wants to play well, so he can show his golf buddies that he is a good golfer and thus a good person. This attitude prevents him from relaxing and focusing on golf.

While pulling the wedge out of my bag to hit the first warm-up shot, I recognize that I'm not very focused. I'm so concerned with who I'm paired with today that I'm analyzing everyone's golf game. My analytical mind can be a double-edged sword. The positive is that I will play a smart game with good course management. The negative is that my observations might work overtime and get in the way of playing golf. So instead of analyzing the games of other players, I decide to focus on my warm-up and prepare to play the opening holes well. To prepare my best, I need to focus on my game plan for the first couple of holes, believe I can play well before I hit my first shot, and focus on execution rather than the details of my swing.

As you can tell, every player has a different mind-set and approach to the start of the round. And no one player is perfect. I see all types of players in my work as a sport psychologist, and no two people have the exact same personality and attitude for golf. I can recognize the players who are able to play well right out of the gate and those players who struggle with their psyche and confidence early in a round. If you want to get off to a good start to a round, it's important to be in the right frame of mind. Gaining momentum early in the round will go a long way toward scoring a breakthrough round and shooting low.

Can you identify with some of the qualities of the players I described above? Let's discuss the positive and negative attributes of each.

- John is a scrapper. He plays well often because of his belief in his ability. A poor warm-up never ruins his confidence. He knows how to get the ball in the hole and compete. He plays great in tournaments because he focuses better under pressure, but he could be a better player if he wanted to.

- Randy's disposition does not let him play his best. He worries about the result—his final score—before he even tees off. He plays on a "confidence roller-coaster." He thinks he must shoot better than one over par on the first three holes if he is going to "earn" some confidence and play well that day. He is left with more doubt than confidence if he doesn't get off to a good start. And it gets worse from there. He plays avoidance golf—trying to avoid hitting bad shots instead of thinking about hitting good shots.

- Rick plays golf to have fun with his buddies. Rick may talk too much during the round for some players. He won't win the tournament, but he will have a good time. Rick does not play golf to shoot low scores, and that's OK.

- Joe plays for the wrong reasons. He plays to earn self-respect, something that is missing in his life. He's too nervous and self-conscious and tries too hard to play well. He's mentally handicapped before he even starts the round.

Many golfers I've worked with have the same obstacle to playing well as Randy and Joe. They just don't give themselves the best chance to start the round off with confidence, composure, and a positive attitude. In order to shoot as low as possible, you must learn how to start the round with confidence and feel some momentum! How can you begin a round with confidence? What are the catalysts for getting off to a good start to shoot a low round? How do the pros start a round off with a bang and get momentum early? If you don't have momentum early in the round, how can you get it? I'll explore these questions in this chapter.

The Power of Momentum

You can't play your best and shoot low without momentum. The feeling of momentum can hit a player fast but leave just as quickly. One minute you might be walking with a bounce in your step after hitting a huge drive—and the very next hole be hanging your head after four-putting. Momentum is psychological, but it begins with the last shot, a previous hole, or solid performance on the last few holes. Just one long putt, a great par save, or a lucky break can get you in the groove. Likewise, just one three-putt, one lost ball, or one bad break can upset the flow.

A couple years ago I was playing golf with three students from the Golf Academy of the South in Orlando, a school where golfers learn about the golf business. I taught a sport psychology class at the school, which included working with students on the course. I'll always remember one particular round I played with my students at Deer Run Golf Course. I didn't get off to a particularly good start because I shot a birdieless 43 on the front side—not a good score, but not a terrible score either. Although the front nine is more difficult than the back nine, I'm sure my students were not impressed with my performance on the first nine.

I started the back nine with a birdie on the easy par-5 10th and immediately felt a rush of confidence. All of a sudden, momentum kicked in and I was playing like a pro. I followed that birdie with a few solid pars in a row and then chipped in for a second birdie. I made a third birdie on number 16 by holing a 40-foot putt to go three under par on the back. I shot a career-low 33 on the back nine with three birdies and six pars to shoot 76, my best score at Deer Run. The 43-33 comeback impressed one of my students. He asked me after the round, "How did you stay so calm and not get upset after the front nine? I would have folded and given up on the round." This was a great lesson for my students. I was glad to teach them by example that good things can happen at any time in the round. You can never give up, pack your bags, or tank a round, because you never know when the power of momentum will jump-start the round.

To get off to a good start in the round, you must create or feel momentum. Momentum is probably the single most important psychological phenomenon that helps all pros go low, such as when David Duval shot 59 at the 1999 Bob Hope. Momentum is not just a phenomenon exclusive to golfers—it happens all the time to athletes in other sports. Momentum may be the most important mental weapon to winning in any sport. What is momentum and how do you get it? Both a tour pro and an amateur feel momentum similarly. Momentum is that feeling of having a bounce in your step; you feel like you are walking on clouds, or you're "on a roll" and Lady Luck is with you. An amateur gets momentum in a different manner than a tour pro does. An amateur gains momentum when she strings together three solid pars in a row, hits that big drive, or sinks a long putt to save par. A pro feels momentum when he makes three birdies in a row, sinks an eagle putt, or chips in for birdie.

Momentum is a close brother to confidence. Without confidence, you are left with doubt, indecision, and a lack of momentum. Confidence is simply the feeling that you can play well. You feel confident when you stand over a ball in the fairway and you know that you can execute well and hit the ball on the green. Momentum starts with the confidence you gained from making a solid par or sinking a long putt to save par on the first hole. It's the feeling you had when you opened a round with three straight pars and can't wait to get to the next hole. I look at momentum as "confidence squared." When you have momentum, you've had confidence for a few shots in a row or over a stretch of holes. It's a sort of confidence track record—"I've played well on holes one, two, three, and four. No reason for it to stop now. I'm on a roll; it's my day"—that stays with you on the next shot or next hole.

The Start of Something Big

Many catalysts spark momentum. Most often, momentum kicks in when you make a few solid pars, hole out a chip shot, or string together three solid holes. Sometimes, all it takes to create momentum is a great shot or a long putt that falls in the cup. This is exactly what happened to Chip Beck when he shot his 59. On the first hole of the third round of the 1991 Las Vegas Invitational, Chip sank a 40-foot putt for birdie, and this was the catalyst that jump-started his round.

However, Beck's quest for 59 started long before the third round of the Vegas event. About six months before the tournament, Chip's wife planted the thought about shooting 59, which started Chip thinking about the possibility. Chip's wife predicted that he would be the next player to cross this barrier. She told him he was going to win the million-dollar bonus established a few years earlier by Hilton Hotels for anyone who shot 59 or better. Half a million would go to the player's charity of choice and the other half to the player. Chip's reply to his wife was that he didn't know if he would do it, but somebody was going to earn that bonus money. The conversations he had with his wife about shooting a 59 settled well in his mind. He started thinking it was possible, feeling it was possible . . . to shoot a 59! The genesis of a great round had already been set in action six months before, helping Chip believe he could shoot the second 59 in PGA Tour history.

The events leading up to the tournament were also instrumental in helping Chip prepare to shoot a low score. Just two weeks before the Las Vegas event, Chip played in the 1991 Ryder Cup. He hit the ball well, but he didn't score well. His putter let him down. After the Ryder Cup he took a week off to rest up for the Las Vegas Invitational, but going into the tournaments he was still riding an emotional high from playing in the Ryder Cup.

Ironically, the week of the Las Vegas event fellow players opened Chip's mind further to the possibility of shooting a low round. All week, tour players were talking about how someone could easily shoot a 59 on the Las Vegas course. With all the talk on the putting green about low scores and the encouragement from his wife, Chip believed now more than ever in his ability to shoot a 59. Shooting 59 was more than remotely possible now—it was inevitable. In my view, the events leading up to the third round of the Las Vegas Invitational—the discussion with his wife and fellow players talking about shooting a 59—helped Chip step into the record book. One thing is for sure: Chip believed in his skills enough to shoot 59.

Chip had broken 60 in his mind before he shot the second 59 in PGA Tour history. If you want to break 90, 80, or 70 for the first time, you must first believe in your skills to do so.

Beck did not start the third round of the Vegas event particularly well. On the very first hole he hit a poor drive into the rough. His second shot wasn't much better: he hit a fat 7-iron on the front of the green 40 feet from the pin. But on the next shot his fate changed. He drained that 40-footer for birdie, which he reacted to like an intravenous injection of confidence. He said, "I had a 40-footer, and when it went right into the middle of the hole floodgates opened up—it was like wow! That's what got me going. Right then it was a complete turnaround. The hole got bigger and I felt like I was going to make putts. It was amazing. I felt it right then at that time—I thought 'Oh, that's really different.' I had so many long putts at the Ryder Cup, and I didn't make any of them. I hit good putts, but they didn't go in. And that one went in—that changed my whole psychology!" And the rest is now history.

Chip turned that one putt into a sign that he was ready to conquer the greens and the course. Many players would have just written it off as a lucky putt and not thought twice about it. But Chip used that one shot as a catalyst to jump-start his round and gather momentum. It's my experience that the great players in the world use moments like this to boost confidence, spark their round, and create a mind-set to go low.

John Huston is no stranger to going low. At the 1998 United Airlines Hawaiian Open he broke the PGA Tour 72-hole scoring record with a 28-under-par 260 performance. He shot rounds of 63-65-66-66 to win by seven strokes, which was the largest margin of victory on the PGA Tour in 1998. It broke a scoring record that had stood for 53 years. John considers himself a "streaky" player, one who either plays great or plays mediocre. When he is on, as was the case in Hawaii, he can light it up and lap the field. If he doesn't bring his A game to the course, he may miss the cut. John's career-low round came at the 1996 Memorial Tournament when he shot a course-record 61, beating the next-best score that day by four shots.

For most tour pros, good scoring comes down to making putts.

Many players hit it great from tee to green. The winner's check usually goes to the player who is draining putts. And when a player like John Huston starts draining putts early in the round, the confidence he gains helps him catch on fire. So making putts early is a key that helps most players catch momentum. Huston said, "If you make two birdies early to get to a couple under par, it feels like you can feed off of that. You got a little bit of a cushion if you happen to make a bogey. I would say especially if you make a couple of good putts, there's nothing like seeing a putt go in, knowing that you can make some putts that day."

As is the case with other players, what helps Huston gain confidence is the feeling of good rhythm in his swing and putting stroke early. Not all, but most "feel players" on tour rely on good feelings in their swing to be confident. Robert Damron, for example, feels confident when he has good rhythm in his swing before he goes to the first tee. He said, "Some mornings when you start warming up and you know you've got it, there's a good chance you could play well that day, confidence builds from that point. . . . There are some days I will tell you—look out—before I get on the first tee." John Huston, also a feel player, draws confidence early from good rhythm, which feeds his momentum. "I think the most important thing in golf is rhythm. You get into a nice rhythm with your putting stroke or your swing, then you just start feeling confident." Rhythm gives John that added confirmation that he is ready to hit good shots and make putts. It makes the game easier, because he doesn't have to work at finding it.

> *The key is to get the ball in play and give yourself*
> *opportunities at birdie. Then, when you make a couple of*
> *putts, stay out of your own way.*
> —JOHN HUSTON

An average golfer can get momentum after holing a long putt for par to make three solid pars in a row, but tour pros get momentum when they make three birdies in a row or go eagle, birdie, eagle. Grant Waite is another example of a player who used momentum to shoot a career low—his 60 in the final round of the 1996 Phoenix Open. Grant shot seven under par on his first nine. He started the back nine with three straight pars on holes 10 to 12, the most difficult holes for Grant on the course. Tough holes can be just as intimidating for a seasoned tour pro as for an amateur. A tough hole can be a tight driving hole, a long hole with water down the side, a hole that doesn't play to your strength, or a hole you may have had trouble with in the past. Even though Grant knew he needed a low round to make up some ground on the field, he was happy to par the first three holes because he knew that he could make up ground on the remaining holes.

Grant started with a flurry, making eagle at 13, birdie at 14, and another eagle at 15. After the second eagle, his momentum and confidence skyrocketed. "It's a feeling of knowing things are going your way—'Today is my day; let's go.' The further I got into the round, the more I was thinking that this is going to be my day. My confidence level got higher and higher throughout the day to where it got beyond my having any doubt at all. . . . The better I started to play, the more I believed it was going to be my day, and the more I believed in myself that I was going to shoot a low score," Grant said about the round. After eagle, birdie, eagle, he then birdied 16 and 17 and parred 18. At that point he thought shooting 59 was a real possibility, with several birdie holes on the front side.

I think his attitude before the round helped set up his mind-set to go low. Before Sunday's round, he was hitting the ball great in warm-up. Grant commented to his caddie, "We aren't doing so well in the tournament. I'm hitting the ball well today—let's see how low we can shoot." The thought was implanted in his mind to shoot a low number. He didn't have a target score—67, for example. His goal was to try to birdie every hole and get momentum on his side. He was in 63rd position at the start of the day and had nothing to lose by being aggressive. Finishing back in the pack would earn him a small check. He could pass a lot of players by shooting seven or eight under, which would give him a chance at earning a larger check that week. He got to 11 under par and stood on the 16th tee needing only one more birdie to shoot 59, but he parred the last three holes and shot 60. He had two good chances on 17 and 18 to make birdie, but he burned the edge of the cup with both putts. He passed about 60 players in the field and finished in the top 10.

To play well, you first must be confident in your ability to play, rather than wait to play well so you can be confident. The sport psychology adage "you must believe before you can achieve" was certainly true for both Chip Beck and Grant Waite. This is a great definition of confidence, but when it comes to confidence there are varying degrees of it. Confidence is based on the strength of one's conviction to perform a task. It can range from no confidence to complete confidence in any given task. The language you use to describe confidence is another way to look at the strength of your conviction. I talk about four levels. The first level is "*Maybe* I can do this." The second is "I *think* I can do this." The third is "I *know* I can do this." And the fourth is "I *will* do this." Most amateurs fluctuate between the first two levels of confidence—"Maybe" and "I think I can," which are not as strong a belief as "I know" or "I will." The most important catalyst to a great round is your belief in your golf skills and ability to score. How much do you believe it's possible to break 90, 80, 70, or whatever your personal threshold may be? Do you think about it often enough to make it become a reality? If you think you can break 90 for the first time, you have a better chance to do it.

Momentum can also come swiftly when you get a good break, such as when your ball hits the side of a bunker and kicks down close to the pin. It's the feeling "I'm lucky today" or "The gods are on my side; it must be my day." Steve Jones, like many other players, feeds off momentum and believes luck plays an important role. Steve won the 1997 Phoenix Open by 11 shots over Jesper Parnevik. He shot 26 under par with rounds of 62, 65, 65, and 67, which at that time was one shy of a PGA Tour 72-hole scoring record. He shot a 16-under 126 for the first two rounds, tying the PGA Tour record for the best 36 holes to start a tournament. The first round in which he shot 62 was a career-low round. He had momentum on his side early in the round, which helped him get to five under after 10.

It's funny how luck can be a catalyst to shooting a low round (or keeping a low round going), which can alter the outcome. Jones told me that "how the ball bounces" makes a big difference. One fortunate bounce, a lip-in instead of a lip-out, or a lucky kick off of a tree can keep a great round alive and keep momentum going. One lucky shot or putt can give you the feeling that "it's my day" or "this is my tournament to win." Steve Jones said, "It's easier to keep the momentum when you get a good break and not a bad break and make a bogey. Momentum is huge whenever you are playing well; you are trying to keep momentum on your side. And the days when I've had a good round going—say, six under after 10 holes—if I lose my momentum after a bogey, I might end up just three under for the day after getting it to six early."

> *Every day is different. If it's your tournament to win, you*
> *will win—that's what I believe.*
>
> —Steve Jones

When you're good, you're lucky, which applies to golf. When you are playing well, you're probably quick to notice only good breaks, such as an off-line approach shot that bounces off the side of a bunker and rolls next to the pin. You never see bad breaks when playing well. Even when you do notice a bad break, you quickly ignore it. Look for the good breaks that happen, and don't think that bad breaks are an omen for bad golf to come.

The opposite happens when you are playing poorly. You see every little mishap as a bad break. "I'm just not lucky today," you say to yourself after the ball hits a hard spot on the green and bounces over into the rough. Whether you see good breaks or bad breaks, how you perceive luck or misfortune becomes a self-fulfilling prophecy. If you think it's your day to play well because of a fortunate bounce or a good run of holes, this serves to boost confidence. Likewise, if you think "it's not my day" when your ball rests in a divot in the middle of the fairway, it can hurt your confidence.

The Hazards of Momentum

You would think that momentum could only help you shoot low. Most people would argue that there are not many negatives to momentum. What, if any, are the risks of gaining momentum early?

With confidence and momentum comes exhilaration. This is a positive emotion, but if it's not contained, it can lead to mental errors. The excitement or thrill of playing well causes the release of adrenaline in the bloodstream. You get a boost of energy and you feel pumped up, juiced, and focused. This can be a very positive feeling for pros who are playing well, but the additional boost of energy must be accounted for.

David Duval's 59: 59 Is Like Pitching a Perfect Game

Coming into the 1999 Bob Hope Chrysler Classic, David Duval had won nine of his last 28 tournaments. He was on a roll and full of confidence. In the first four rounds of the pro-am tournament, Duval played with other sports stars, including Emmitt Smith, Marcus Allen, Pete Sampras, and Roger Clemens. Come Sunday, Duval was the only star in the sky. Even so, before the final round, Duval lagged seven strokes behind the leaders. He felt "tapped out" on the range during his warm-up. It had been a long week, and after all, seven shots back, he didn't think he had a chance to win. On the first tee, his lethargy disappeared.

On the first hole, Duval hit a pitching wedge to five feet and made birdie. He birdied holes two and three as well. After two-putting for par on number four, he birdied number five, then parred six, seven, and eight. He finished the front side with another birdie for a score of 31—not quite a historic front side, but good enough to gain momentum and confidence for the back nine. "When you are turning five under, 59 is kind of out of the question, really. You don't expect to pick up eight shots in nine holes," Duval would later say. He birdied numbers 10, 11, and 12 to quickly get to eight under par.

He saved the best for last. After two-putting from 12 feet on number 13, Duval birdied 14, 15, and 16, then parred 17. On the par-five finishing hole, he hit a 5-iron to within six feet for a chance at eagle. Now the real pressure was on. It wasn't a 30-footer for eagle—it was in "gimme" range given the way he was putting. To help matters, Duval got a good read from Bob Tway's putt. He went through his normal routine, took a couple of deep breaths, looked at the hole, and hit the putt. It fell in.

Five under on the last five holes is great scoring any day, but to do it with the chance of shooting 59 and winning the tournament requires total focus and composure. Even his playing partners were impressed. "He knocked down flagsticks all day," said an amazed Bob Tway. Duval shot a 59 and had only 53 feet of one-putts combined, with the longest putt being 10 feet. It was probably the best ball-striking round in his career. "It's like pitching a perfect game. . . . Everything has to go your way," Duval said.

The first-tee jitters are a good example of the effects of adrenaline on your thoughts and physiological state. The excitement and anticipation to get the game started cause several mental and bodily changes. Butterflies in the stomach, sweaty palms, increased heart rate, and faster breathing all result from prematch nerves. Many inexperienced amateur players interpret these reactions as being negative and harmful to their performance, whereas seasoned pros view these feelings of anticipation as helpful. Most worry when pregame butterflies are absent.

The added strength that comes from adrenaline changes how a pro plays golf. Seasoned pros know when to throttle back if the adrenaline bug bites. David Duval, for example, needed eagle on the last hole of the 1999 Bob Hope to shoot 59. Pumped up by the possibility of shooting a 59, he took one less club than he thought was needed for the shot. The rational side of his brain said to hit 4-iron, but his experience told him to hit a 5-iron. He nailed a great 5-iron pin-high eight feet left of the hole, and the rest is history. Amateurs experience the same physiology when psyched up. After you hole two long putts on the back nine to get back to seven over par coming to number 18, the excitement you feel about breaking 80 for the first time becomes both an asset and a liability. The added excitement and adrenaline help you focus better, but you must account for the influence of adrenaline or you will fly the green.

Billy Mayfair is very familiar with the effects of momentum on a player when she is going low. Billy considers himself a "steady player," posting a lot of 68s and 69s but not many 61s—only one, to be exact. So going low is different for Billy than, say, for John Huston, who lights it up often. Billy, like many other players, thinks the downside to momentum is getting too pumped up, which causes him to hit the ball farther than normal. For someone who doesn't shoot low often, adrenaline makes it more difficult to pick the right club. "The hard thing about momentum is that you start to hit the ball farther. I was hitting it one or two clubs farther. You are pumped up and your swing is right on, and you are just firing at every pin," Billy recalls. It's sort of a good problem to have, but one that you need to be cognizant of when you are riding the wave of momentum.

We have discussed how confidence soars to new heights when momentum kicks in, but can it soar out of control? For some amateur players, momentum can swell into overconfidence, which turns a potential breakthrough round into an average round. A sudden rush of momentum can make a golfer feel like Superman or Superwoman. This is similar to the "gladiator effect" for football players. The player develops a feeling of invincibility because he's crawled out of the pile unscathed so many times before. A golfer's tendency when overconfident is to step outside of his or her abilities, abandon smart golf, and play foolishly. Instead of laying up on par 5s that you can't reach, your ego says go for it. Rather than chipping out of the woods, you try a fantasy shot over and around the trees because you are "on a roll and nothing is going to stop you." Instead of prudently using a 3-wood or iron to hit fairways on tight holes, you start to smash driver on every hole because you're invincible. Overconfidence can turn a smart, conservative player into a dumb, attack-without-reason player.

Ernie Els is an example of a player who can post low numbers while playing within his capabilities. He has shot both 61 and 62 three times in his career, with several rounds in the middle 60s. One

61 came during the second round of the 1995 GTE Byron Nelson Classic, when he shot 10 under par at Cottonwood Valley. He shot 69-61-65-68 to win his second PGA Tour title. Els knows the importance of exercising discipline when momentum is working. He thinks that no golfer, regardless of ability, should play with reckless abandon even when running on all cylinders. A golfer needs the discipline to throttle back and play percentage golf, especially when the voice of confidence says go for it. "It's an aggressive patience. You still must hit the percentage shot, but it's an aggressive shot," says Els.

When you get off to a good start, you have to keep momentum in check and not get carried away by overconfidence. If you play bogey golf and start the round with three consecutive pars, the early confidence is an advantage, but overenthusiasm can work against you. Golf is not like a track-and-field event, in which play is over very quickly. It doesn't matter if a sprinter gets juiced after the race—that particular event is over—but in golf you still have three hours of golf left to play. Foolish exuberance can cause you to make a dumb decision, which can reverse the fast start you had on the first three holes. Tour players try to stay emotionally balanced. This means you shouldn't get too excited (or overconfident) about starting with three pars or get too down about making three double bogeys in a row.

Even the best players in the world don't let momentum go to their heads. Knowing limitations is one area where professionals are superior to amateurs. Even when David Duval has his A game, he knows when to play to the center of the green or lay up on par 5s. If you watched him shoot 59, you could tell from his reaction after making a birdie that he didn't get too excited. He stayed calm and in control the entire round. You can make a high number and lose momentum by firing at every flag, hitting driver on every hole, and charging every putt when you have early momentum. Before every round, tour pros have a strategy for playing the course. You, too, should have a strategy for playing a particular course that is geared around your strengths and capabilities. Your strategy and shot selection should not change, especially when you are in the middle of shooting a low round. In Chapter 9, I'll come back to course management.

Ernie Els, on his way to a 10-under-par round, got to six under par through 11 holes. Realizing he was in the middle of a great round, his goal was to keep the good round going and not back up by making a mental error. He still had to play high-percentage shots, even when playing his best. Ernie takes the trouble around the greens out of play by playing to the fat side of the green when necessary and letting his putter do the talking. Keeping the ball in play, hitting greens, and giving himself opportunities to make birdie—not opportunities to save bogey—was the plan. When he had the opportunity to take dead aim at the flag with a short iron, he did. But he didn't take dead aim on every hole. Every course you play, you'll find two or three "sucker" pin placements. Sucker pins are pins that are positioned close to the edge of the green where an errant shot can cause a very difficult up and down or a penalty shot. Els knows when to avoid these pins and play, for example, six paces left of a flag that is tucked on the right side of the green. "You build on the momentum. Don't back off; never back off. I think that's the key—you have to play fearless, but still play percentage golf," says Els.

Catching Momentum Early

The best way to catch a wave of momentum early is to start the round with confidence. I don't want you to make the same mental errors that cause Randy and Joe to shoot high scores. What can you do to get off to a good start and in position to ride momentum all the way to the clubhouse?

1. Prepare yourself mentally by believing you can play well. Randy can play well only if he starts the round well. David Duval doesn't wait until he hits a good shot or makes a birdie before he feels confident. He takes confidence with him to the first tee, which gives him the best chance to succeed. You can feel confident by recalling past success (even if sparse or long ago), using your experience, believing in your ability, and picturing success. Recall one or two events from the past to make you feel confident now,

such as a good round, a productive practice session, or a stretch of holes where you played well.

2. Expectations are your worst enemy. Randy makes the mistake of expecting too much from himself early in the round. It's an absolute must for him to play well on the opening holes. That type of thinking is his downfall. If he doesn't play up to his expectations, he feels like a failure immediately, which hurts his confidence for the rest of the round.

3. Use knowledge of good course management to your advantage. If you are preparing to play in a tournament, play a practice round and study the course. Check the yardage plates to the center of the green, pick smart targets from the tee box, and select the clubs you will use off the tees. Develop a game plan to play the course based on your strengths. For example, know the best distance for your third shot into the par-5 holes. In Chapter 9, you'll learn more about course management when going low.

4. Don't concern yourself with a poor warm-up. Many players don't focus their best until they get on the course, when the competitive juices start to flow. Focus on getting loose and relaxed for the opening holes. Don't let a poor warm-up dampen your confidence for the round. Instead, think about the last time you hit the ball well in practice.

5. Take advantage of good shots. You don't have to sink a 40-footer on the first hole, à la Chip Beck, to get momentum, but you can pat yourself on the back when you make a good shot early in the round and use it as a sign of good things to come.

6. Focus on the first tee shot and your plan for playing the first holes rather than being too concerned with your final score. You can't break 90 on the first tee. The only thing you should think about is how to best get the first tee shot into the fairway. Your score will take care of itself when you play each shot to the best of your ability, but first you must take care of business on the first tee and get the ball into play.

7. Don't jump to conclusions by making false generalizations about your golf game. Making false generalizations based on one or two past events is not rational or healthy for your game. Just because you've played poorly once before on the course you are playing today does not mean you will play poorly repeatedly on that course.

8. At the start of the round, focus on executing good shots—don't try to avoid hitting bad shots. One of the biggest errors amateurs make is an obsession with avoiding negative consequences. You can be sure that Tiger Woods did not start the last round of the 1997 Masters thinking about avoiding embarrassment by not blowing a nine-shot lead. That's a fearful, protective way to play golf. Tiger increased his lead the last day of the 1997 Masters and won by a Masters-record 12 shots. See the ball going to your target and focus on that image.

9. Stay confident if you get off to a shaky start in a round. You are the only person who can turn a bad start into a bad round. Don't assume that a bad start is an omen for the rest of the round.

Regaining Momentum When It's Lost

When you are playing with momentum, golf seems easy. You're making solid pars, holing putts you don't usually make, and saving par. Confidence carries you. But golf is more difficult when you don't have momentum to carry you early in the round. Many good players struggle early in the round, for different reasons. You might not get focused until the middle of the round. You might not feel any confidence until you hit a good shot. How do you handle yourself when your game is in neutral or when you don't have momentum early in the round? This is the time to create your own momentum.

How can you catch momentum when you don't have it? The double bogey you made on the second hole is defeating your attitude. To turn the round around and create momentum, you must start somewhere. The double you made is in the past and influences the next tee shot only if you carry it with you. It's hard to play golf with a "monkey on the back." Every shot and every hole is a new opportunity to turn your game around. If you continue to be fatalistic, you may never make that first par. Break your round down into 18 separate games. When one hole is over, it's on to the next game with a fresh attitude, ready to take on the challenge of a new hole. Tell yourself: "On this hole, I'm going to play like I know I can!"

Remember that bad breaks are just a fluke and not a bad omen. Bad breaks are not a sign that you are unlucky today. Don't talk yourself into thinking, "I'm just not lucky today." This type of thinking can ruin the chances of getting any momentum, because you are now looking for or expecting bad breaks to happen. Luck is a part of golf—even pro golfers such as Steve Jones would agree. You can't control good or bad luck, but you can control how you respond to bad breaks. Write it off as a fluke and get on with the next shot.

Momentum is emotional. You can actually create negative momentum if you have negative emotions early in the round. When you haven't made any pars and are feeling down and out, do you get down on yourself? Pessimism and feelings of despair only accelerate negative momentum. The more you focus on past bogeys and poor putting, the greater the despair. Don't let negative emotions turn into negative momentum.

Final Thoughts

To shoot your best score, it doesn't matter if you are an amateur trying to break 90 for the first time or a pro trying to shoot in the low 60s—momentum and confidence are strong catalysts in each case. Most golfers blow their chances of shooting a low score even before they get on the first tee. Confidence is not just a by-product of playing good golf today. Confidence both precedes and follows good golf. Don't mentally handicap yourself by doubting your ability, worrying about what score you can shoot, or focusing on what others think about you or your game. Forget about what others may or may not think if you duff a shot. Focus your mind on hitting your best shot, seeing the shot in your mind, and concern yourself with the best plan to par each hole. This way, you will allow yourself the opportunity to see good results and ride a wave of momentum all the way to the clubhouse.

Transcending Mechanics in the Zone

Any golfer who plays well down the stretch is playing without any mechanical thoughts, putting or otherwise.

—JOHN HUSTON (SET PGA TOUR'S ALL-TIME 72-HOLE SCORING RECORD WITH A 28-UNDER-PAR 260)

Learning to drive a car for the first time can be awkward. Coordinating the steering wheel, gas pedal, and brake demand your complete attention. All the more so with a manual transmission, because of the concentration needed to coordinate the gas pedal with the clutch. Remember how the car jumped and then rocked when you popped the clutch too fast? Driving felt clumsy at best, but as you did it more you gradually controlled the pedals and steering wheel with little or no effort. You felt the movements of the car as you pressed the gas pedal and turned the wheel.

This "feel" approach to driving allowed you to focus solely on the road ahead and react to the surroundings. Soon you felt confident and in control. The process of learning to drive is similar to beginning any new sport, golf included. The precise and coordinated movements of a competent golfer replace the awkward feelings when you first began to play golf, but not without considerable practice. Of all sporting skills, golf may be the hardest to pick up naturally. Young children learn how to throw, kick, run, and jump, which seem like very natural skills to perform. But golf is a different package of skills altogether.

As your golf skills evolve, you pass through three distinct stages of learning. When first learning to putt, for example, you pick up or are taught the fundamentals. Stage one requires you to grasp the basics of the stroke, including the grip, stance, setup, and stroke path. It's a lot to digest initially. The initial "how to" of putting (stroke, path, etc.) requires a very voluntary and deliberate mind-set. The skills for reading greens and visualization are to come later— you aren't ready for them at first.

With continued practice of the proper grip, setup, and putting stroke, you gain confidence with repetition. In stage two, you don't have to work on the fundamentals as much. You can use the proper grip and get into a stance with ease, but the stroke still demands concentration. With more repetition, the stroke begins to feel effortless. That's when feel and vision start to develop. Finally, you reach stage three, in which you putt competently and the ball starts to drop.

This stage feels like throwing darts: You can look at the target and just throw the dart there. You don't need to think about *how* to throw the dart. With putting, no conscious thought about *how* to make a stroke is necessary. Reading the green properly, seeing the line, and feeling the right speed of the putt are now more important. A mechanistic and conscious approach to putting is replaced with a feel-based and imaginative process to putting. In this stage, stroking the ball should feel effortless and automatic, freeing your mind to focus on the target or the speed of the putt.

Understanding the learning process is important to playing your best golf. I'm sure you have experienced and can identify with all the stages of learning. Anytime you make a change in your swing, you revert to a mind-set similar to the earlier stage of learning. Ideally, when playing, you want to perform with a feel-based, non-conscious mind-set, which I'll discuss later in this chapter. Once you get to that feel-based stage, any effort to overcontrol the swing or putting stroke (a condition in which you become a learner again, rather than a performer) is counterproductive to playing your best.

Playing Consciously Outside "The Zone"

Henry has just finished a lesson with his teaching pro and is excited about testing the lesson on the course. His instructor gave some solid suggestions that helped him hit better on the range. Before his teacher says goodbye, he tells Henry to practice the changes diligently. Eager to see results, however, Henry heads off to the first tee. He takes a few practice swings, thinking about what he has just been told in the lesson. It all seems to make sense, and Henry's swing feels comfortable.

Confident that he will drive one cleanly down the fairway, Henry addresses the ball. As he starts into his backswing, time seems to stop. Henry freezes up, unable to pull the trigger. What has happened?

Henry was so busy reviewing a checklist of what he was supposed to do, it became nearly impossible for him to start the backswing. It was all so clear on the range, but on the tee he strained to remember everything his pro had told him. "Stay balanced, smooth takeaway, low and slow, don't lunge at the ball," Henry said to himself repeatedly, like a mantra. The instructor's words were still fresh in his mind, but he couldn't process everything, and mild panic set in. It felt like the last time he crammed all night for a test in college and his mind went blank when he sat down to take the test.

"Just hit it," Henry commanded himself. He started the club back, his swing cues repeating themselves. He made an uncoordinated, quick swing that produced the wicked slice he had before the lesson. "Just need a few swings to warm up," he told himself, but 18 holes later he had not found the groove yet and he wondered what happened.

Henry is typical of many golfers I have met in my travels. They sabotage their performance with too many thoughts about how to swing the club while playing. See, Henry does not have a clue about how much practice is needed to make a swing change. He thinks that once his instructor "fixed" his slice on the range, he would hit every shot well—or at least better than he did before the lesson. He did not know that his swing couldn't change in one lesson without repeated practice. He was educated about how to make corrections, but then told that practice was necessary to make the new swing repeatable. And *practice* is the key word here. He was hitting it well on the range because of his teacher's feedback and direction, but that is only temporary—it will last only until he can ingrain the changes.

Henry's other problem is that he forgot golf is a target game, not a mechanical game. To perform his best, he has to play by feel and imagination. Many times he has heard great players like Tiger Woods talk about working on a fundamental such as swing plane with his coach. What he didn't hear was that Tiger works on his swing plane in practice off the course, not while playing. On the course, Tiger is into the target and thinking about a feeling that will create the shot he wants to hit. He doesn't focus on the mechanical changes he has made with his coach when he plays golf.

In order to score your best every day and make a breakthrough round, you must first pass through these three stages of learning. Once you get to stage three, you are now capable of playing target golf, which is a major component of playing in the zone. Playing in the zone is what helps golfers of all ability score their best—and what will help you make a scoring breakthrough.

Playing Unconsciously in "The Zone"

If you have played in what professional golfers call "the zone," you know what it feels like to free your mind from the conscious effort of making a swing and instead play target golf, even if it was only for a few holes. An uncluttered, calm mind is essential to playing in the zone. You stifle the chance of entering the zone when you think too much about swing mechanics. Golfers often describe the feeling of the zone as playing unconscious, automatic, or athletic golf. You still must calculate the distance to the target, pick a target, and plan the shot; but mainly your focus is on the flight of the ball or the feeling of a good shot. In the zone, you transcend mechanics. Thus, performance feels effortless, as if no thought is required to execute good shots.

*You let the lessons and everything that you practice take
care of themselves. When out on the golf course, you're just
focusing on your target.*

—MEG MALLON

Grant Waite has always worked very hard on his mechanics, but
early in his career he never really believed enough in his swing to let
go of the mechanics and be confident. He spent many hours video-
taping his swing, breaking it down piece by piece, analyzing it with
his instructor or another player, and trying to make it perfect. This
helped him acquire a reputation of having one of the best swings on
the Tour. Yet he's had only one win on the PGA Tour, the 1993
Kemper Open.

During his final round of 60 in the 1996 Phoenix Open, with the
help of his instructor, he was able to let go of mechanics and just
play golf. During this round, he found himself in a unique state of
total focus without trying. He said, "It was a feeling of immense
calm, because I had gone beyond nervousness. I really had the belief
that I was going to shoot in the 50s. If you can reach that point
where you totally convince yourself that you can do it, then all the
nervousness and anxiety leave and it's a state of total focus without
trying to focus. Your mind is right into what you are doing."

Waite will tell you himself that earlier in his career he was pre-
occupied with the mechanics of his swing. Shooting 60 showed him
how to rely more on his athletic ability instead of trying to make
a perfect swing every shot. "You have to have the serenity to see
your shot and allow your athletic ability to come through to play
the shot. You have to get out of your own way and let it happen,"
he said.

*It's just natural to forget about all the mechanics when you
start playing well. That's what everybody should do anyway.*

—JOHN HUSTON

Waite used an interesting metaphor to express the abandonment
of mechanics. He said he felt that he was out on the golf course
"painting" the best strokes of his life. "The artistic expression of

what the game is all about is beyond trying or looking at things as good or bad. You get beyond trying to win or lose, trying to concentrate, trying with swing mechanics, or trying to do everything right. You are just playing with artistic expression," Waite concludes. He has learned to let the mechanics of his game take a backseat to a belief in his natural ability, a realization that was long in coming. You, too, can let go of your mechanical self and instead play golf with your creative instincts in command. Your mechanics probably are not as good as Grant Waite's, and I'm sure you don't practice as much as a professional does, but you still have to take your best swing to the course, which is your natural ingrained swing.

I had a very encouraging conversation with Grant Waite at the 1999 Greater Hartford Open. We talked about the best way to practice at his level. "What's the purpose of practice?" he asked. I said, simply, "To develop confidence so you can do it on the course." He said, "Right, but how do you develop confidence?" I said through repetition and seeing desired results. Waite replied, "You can't rely on results." What Grant meant was that players become too obsessed with getting good results on the practice tee, which can deteriorate confidence if it's poor practice. What's more important is to ingrain the correct feeling of the golf swing.

He went on to say that golf is not about contemplating swing positions, where the right elbow is at the top, for example. The real goal of practice is to set up each shot with a feeling, refine that feeling, and use the same feeling to produce a good shot. He demonstrated how he could simply set up to a shot with the feeling of a fade and then hit the fade successfully. See the shot, feel the swing, and hit it. He showed me how he could see a draw holding into a left-to-right wind, feel the shot, and hit the draw successfully. This was a great example of playing artistic and athletic golf, and I have been happy to see that he has made real progress with this part of the game.

The Golfer as Spectator

When Ted Tryba was in college, he got the lesson of his life while playing a round of golf with the best golfer in the world, Jack Nicklaus. He, Nicklaus, and tour pro Jerry Kelly were playing together, and Ted and Jerry got Jack angry. Ted, after playing the front nine in tough conditions, was two under. Jerry had shot one under and Jack had shot two over. Kelly turned to Tryba and said, "We've got the old man now, Trybs; we'll just bury him on this back side." Jack looked at him with an icy stare that said, Who are you calling old? Ted turned into a spectator on the back nine as Jack turned it on and birdied 10, 11, 12, and 13. Jack also birdied 15 and 16 to shoot 30 on the back nine for a 68. Ted, amazed with Jack's performance, ended up shooting even par on the back for a 72. "It was a crucial day in my life, because I felt like I would never be good enough to play professionally. Jack decided to turn it on, and he did, and he made it look easy. I was in awe," Tryba said.

Ted realized he could play professional golf successfully after he joined the Tour in 1990. Five years later, he won the 1995 Anheuser-Busch Golf Classic. He won again in 1999 at the FedEx St. Jude Classic. Ted recorded the round of his life when he shot an impressive 61 at Riviera Country Club in the 1999 Los Angeles Open. Before the third round, his only goal was to get off to a good start. He did just that by shooting a four-under-par 30 on the front nine. He went on to shoot a 31 on the back nine, which included a birdie-eagle-birdie-birdie-birdie-birdie run starting at number 10. He had a chance to shoot 59 as he came to Riviera Country Club's famous 18th, his last hole. He hit an approach shot long, however, and was faced with having to chip in to shoot 59. His attempt stopped eight feet short of the hole, and his par putt slipped past the hole.

> *It seems that even on the toughest courses, players become unconscious.*
>
> —TED TRYBA

According to Tryba, when you are hitting the ball well, your score boils down to how well you can concentrate. "If I go out on the first five holes and I know I'm hitting it pure, I know I'm going to have a good back side. All I have to do is concentrate. My back-nine score is determined by how well I select clubs based on the yardage for approach shots and how good of a read I get on my putts," Tryba said. As things turned out that day, he got great looks and enjoyed one of his best putting days ever. He was able to see his lines as if they just popped out of the greens.

Tryba was definitely in the zone that day in L.A. His game felt easy and in control. He didn't labor over club selection or struggle to read the greens. Everything seemed to fall into place. "You're just thinking right because everything seems easy for you—not too many things to think about. When you get good numbers [yardage] for club selection, it's just easy. Good numbers made my decisions quick and decisive. So I never had a chance to question myself." It's that feeling of comfort and serenity that made Ted feel so calm. He explained that this day he was his own spectator, as if he were watching it happen before him. "I was focused, but it was like I was at a distance from the situation. It was easy to get there, to get focused. I could almost watch myself hit each shot like I could look at the ball and make the shot happen just by imagining myself swinging the club."

Tommy Tolles had a similar experience when he shot a career-low round of 62 at the Nike Knoxville Open in 1994. Tolles feels that many amateur players sabotage their performances by thinking too much. "Most of the time, we are our own worst enemy," said Tolles, but he wasn't describing his week in Knoxville. "I got everything on my side in that tournament. I know the course. I'm playing well. I'm making a lot of birdies. I'm an aggressive player, better-than-average length, better-than-average putter, and when all those variables add up, there is too much going for me to just say I'm not sure whether I will play well or not," Tolles said. This is a great example of a player who focuses on reasons to succeed.

> *You may have one or two swing thoughts, but when you get on the golf course, you try to fire at the pins and not think about mechanics.*
>
> —Billy Mayfair

Like Tryba, Tolles was able to transcend the mechanics of the game and feel as if he were watching his own performance. "That was one of the few times I can say that I was my own spectator. I got out of my way mentally," Tolles said. One of the biggest challenges for many players, both professional and amateur, is getting too far ahead mentally by thinking about holes yet to play. For Tolles, the difference between playing great and playing well comes down to the ability to play "in the now."

Waite, Tryba, and Tolles have very different games, yet they all know how to transcend mechanics and let their talent come out. They are aware that focusing too much on swing mechanics can kill their chances of entering the zone. Feeling intimidated by a difficult course or a strong opponent can also hinder you from getting into the zone. Steve Lowery knows well how intimidation can affect his golf game. Steve shot a career-low 60 in the final round of the 1998 Buick Challenge. It was the first 60 shot on tour since Grant Waite did it in 1996. Steve got to 10 under par after just 13 holes, and his confidence was skyrocketing. When a player gets in this state of mind, she feels she can birdie every hole. Lowery parred holes 14 through 16 but birdied the final two holes to shoot 12 under par.

Steve's low round was interesting because he had not played well the first three rounds. After shooting even par the third round, he was very disappointed with his performance. He eventually realized that the golf course had intimidated him during those first three rounds. He worried in particular about hitting his ball into the long rough and then not being able to hit an approach shot on the green. Sunday, he made a commitment to himself not to back down. "I told myself I was not going to be intimidated by the golf course, the rough, the wind, or the grain on the greens. I was determined that when that round was over, I would be able to say I had gone out there and done what I was capable of doing, no matter the circumstances," Lowery said.

Playing scared the first three days had caused him to make tentative swings, and he knew it. "You have a choice on every tee box. You are either going to guide it out there or you are going to stand up there and tee it up and rip it. Sunday I made the right choice every time," Lowery said.

Sometimes frustration can push you to make a positive change in attitude. Steve Lowery had grown frustrated and tired of the way he was preparing himself to play. So he prepared differently for Sunday's round after shooting a disappointing 72 on Saturday. Instead of going to the range and working on mechanics, he decided to believe his mechanics were good enough to play well. He said, "I just trusted myself and the talent I have. You have to believe in your ability that you can shoot 60 and that you don't have to work on swing mechanics to shoot a 60—it's inside you, you just got to let it out." Sunday afternoon, he succeeded in letting his talent come out. He came from way back to finish third in the tournament.

Keys to Playing Target Golf

You can see from the above examples that playing unconscious golf leads to low scoring. When I say unconscious, that doesn't mean totally lacking in thought. It means you are focused on each shot, but you are processing information automatically and triggering the swing with a simple image or thought. On days like this, golf doesn't feel like hard work. Playing in the zone, you are focused on the target or the flight of the shot. Scoring is more important than making pretty swings or hitting the longest drive. If you want to shoot lower scores, you need to learn how to play target golf instead of mechanical golf. Here are some tips to help you play target golf and leave the mechanics on the range.

Save the Checklist for Practice Time

The human mind processes only one thought, idea, or piece of information at one time. The term for this is "serial processing." Unless the golfer's mind works this way, multiple thoughts will tend to overwhelm him. Thinking about a recent lesson while on the golf course, as Henry did, burdens the mind and sends unclear signals to the body. If you want to make a free swing, try ingraining the feeling of a good swing during your practice swing, then shift your focus to the target. Understandably, many players feel uncomfortable without at least one swing thought over the ball. There is nothing wrong with swing thoughts, as long as you keep it to one thought.

Mechanics are a distraction. Anything that gets you off your target is a distraction.

—STEVE LOWERY

The purpose of using a swing thought is to initiate the swing, not to control it. You shouldn't use swing cues such as "keep the left elbow straight," to coach yourself. If you have to coach yourself on every shot, do so on the driving range. The best swing thoughts are related to tempo, rhythm, and balance. John Huston, for example, focuses on the rhythm of his swing and putting stroke. When he feels good rhythm, he knows he is on.

See the Target

I always ask my students if they have the ability to see the target in their mind when they are at address and looking down at the ball. If they answer yes, then I know they have the ability to play target golf. For a purely visual player, the image of the target is extremely helpful in that moment before the backswing is triggered. It helps keep target awareness and cuts off distractions like fear or mechanics. Trust me: the image of the target is all that is needed to initiate the swing. In almost every other sport, athletes look at the target when performing. Golf is a rare exception to this rule. But you can learn to "sense" the target in your mind's eye as you pull the trigger. A "feel" player can also use the same technique, but instead of seeing the target, he will sense its location in a kinesthetic way.

See the Shot

The next-best swing cue after seeing the target is to see the shot. This is very similar to seeing the target, but there's more specific information. A good image to use is a string that shapes the flight of the shot. This image is similar to a frozen rope curving in the air. With this image, you see the shape of the shot (its curve and trajectory) as well as the target. The best players are able to simply see the shot they want to play and then execute it using only the image of the shot. I know you don't practice as much as the pros. However, you can still perform using this method, provided you visualize a shot you are capable of playing. If you don't practice or play a draw, you don't want to waste your energy seeing a shot that you can't actually hit. If you play a 15-yard fade on every shot, see that shot, not a perfectly straight shot.

Al Geiberger's 59: All Phases of the Game Come Together

Al Geiberger is a well-known figure in golf, more so for his nickname, "Mr. 59," than for his career wins on the PGA Tour. During the second round of the 1977 Memphis Classic at Colonial Country Club, Geiberger knew the golf gods were on his side. He was unaware that he was about to break golf's version of the four-minute-mile barrier. He started his round on the back nine, shooting a solid 30. As he got further into the round, he started to think that he wasn't going to miss a shot.

The pressure of shooting the first 59 in PGA Tour history was mounting as Geiberger played his second nine. He was hitting the ball better and better as the round progressed. Standing on the sixth tee (his 15th hole), he was 10 under par. He knew he was going low, but he didn't know exactly how low. He thought to himself, "Oh, my gosh, what have I got myself into? I'm so many under par." He didn't stop to count, but the possibility of shooting a 59 crossed his mind and caused him some discomfort. Never before had a tour pro broken 60 in competition. Geiberger tried to settle himself down with comforting words: "You're hitting the ball better every hole, and your putting is perfect. Just pull out all the stops and be aggressive."

Geiberger, a self-confessed conservative player, struggled to push himself to go for broke and try to birdie the last four holes. He hit it down the middle of the fairway and then birdied his 15th hole to go to 11 under par, and the fans were now rallying for a 59, adding to the pressure. He birdied the seventh hole (his 16th) to go to 12 under par. He needed only one more birdie with two holes left to shoot 59. He parred his 17th hole. He hit his approach shot on Colonial Country Club's ninth hole to 10 feet. All day long, he was making putts from everywhere. His round was even more amazing when you consider the difficulty of the course and the greens. The Bermuda greens were very grainy, because they didn't verticut cut them the way they do today. Standing over the 10-footer, Geiberger said to himself, "Whatever you do, don't leave it short." He slammed that birdie putt into the middle of the cup for the first 59 in PGA Tour history.

Reflecting on the round, Geiberger felt that it was unusual for both his long game and his putting to come together on the same day. Typically, they don't both shine at the same time. He had made a small change in his swing that week, nothing out of the ordinary because he was always making minor changes in hopes of finding the missing link. He found the missing link that day. Geiberger later said, "That changed my life a lot. People still refer to that. Just a few weeks ago, Grant Waite almost shot a 59 on the PGA Tour, and they were talking about my 59. Anytime anyone gets close to it, they bring it up. It's a nice tag to have." He went on to win the 1977 Memphis Classic.

Feel the Shot

The third option for a swing cue is to feel the shot you want to play. That doesn't mean feel the mechanics of the shot. What does a good shot feel like to you? Go ahead and close your eyes for a moment and try to capture the feeling of a good shot. One player might say the tempo felt good. Another player might say that it felt solid at impact. And someone else might say that it felt free and loose. We each have a feeling that's particular to our learning style and swing.

Feel players are more in tune with the feelings of a good swing and don't rely on visual images. Use your practice swing as a visual and tactile rehearsal for a good shot. If it didn't feel right, take another one. That's an advantage of golf: you don't have to hit the ball until you are ready. Now carry that feeling into the shot and use it to trigger the swing. A small dose of nonmechanical information is all your body needs to preprogram the swing.

Don't Steer the Shot

If you play scared golf—trying to avoid hitting a shot in the trees, bunker, or water—you'll steer the ball. This is the exact opposite of transcending mechanics. Steering or guiding shots when you see a tight fairway is conscious, controlled golf. In most cases, the tension caused by the fear of hitting a bad shot puts a tether on your swing. If you try to avoid hitting your ball in the trees to the right, what's the effect? You will end up hitting it into those very trees because you "held on" and blocked your release. If not that, then you may overcompensate and hit the ball left by hanging back and flicking the hands at the ball or making some other overcontrolling motion in the swing. Remember, when fear intrudes, the conscious mind will take over the swing and steer the shot. It's what we call performing as a learner instead of a performer.

Practicing for Target Golf

The goal of practice is to develop a repeatable swing so you have confidence you can hit your targets on the course. Practicing the correct swing is paramount. That's why instruction is so important: if you practice the wrong swing, you're just wasting time. I ask players to split their time between working on the swing and practicing target golf. If you spend all your time on the range and the putting green, working on your golf swing and putting stroke, the tendency is to practice them on the golf course. And that's exactly what you want to avoid if your goal is to score your best. Once you have a repeatable golf swing that you have confidence in, you are ready to focus on playing target golf. The following are suggestions for practicing to play target golf.

Learn from One Trusted Instructor

Today, there is an overabundance of technical information on how to swing the club and play golf. Every instructor has his or her own method or philosophy. The likely result is too many options and a lot of confused golfers. Find an instructor whose ideas you like and trust. The more methods (from various teachers or books) you try to combine into practice, the harder it will be to develop a repeatable swing. Stay with one teacher, one method, and one style of teaching.

Learn It, Feel It, See It

I began this chapter by reminding you of when you learned to drive. It came in stages, remember? In the first stage, you performed a skill in response to systematic verbal commands. This happens early in the learning process—including, for a golfer, when swing changes are undertaken. You command yourself how to move the club: "Take the putter back and forward on the target line." The second stage comes after you learn the basics and can begin to feel the correct movement. Instead of consciously controlling the putterhead back and forth down the line, you have an image (or feeling) of how that stroke feels. You perform by recalling the image and letting your body do the rest. The third stage arrives when you simply can look at the target (the putting line or hole in this case) and have your body respond without conscious effort. After mastering a skill such as putting, the image of the target (or line) is the only input the body needs to make the putt. Vision and imagination go to work, and no conscious control is necessary. This is the best state to play golf in—the stage that will allow you to go low.

To summarize, you learn the correct movement in stage one, you develop the feel of the movement in stage two, and you perform by seeing and/or feeling the target in stage three. How much you play and practice your golf will influence what stage you are in. The closer you can get to stage three when you do practice, the more you are practicing target golf. At the very least, you should translate conscious verbal commands into a "feeling" of a solid swing or putting stroke. This level brings you one step closer to playing target golf.

Shut Off the Conscious Mind

Part of practice should be devoted to conscious swing analysis and part to free-form target practice. What do I mean? In a learning mode, when the goal is to improve your swing, your cognitive mind is very active. You are very conscious of positions of the club during the swing. You are self-analyzing the swing and making judgments about how well you are doing. Your mind is busy comparing the outcome of each swing to the desired outcome. You correct as you go and give yourself verbal commands on how to make the right swing.

Target golf practice is less analytical, less judgmental, and less conscious. The goal is to rely on what you have practiced and trust that you can make an effective swing. You shut down the conscious, trying mind and let your vision and feel take over. This style of practice is more specific to what you must do on the golf course to score your best. Your focus should be on the target instead of the swing, the feel and tempo of the swing instead of path or positions. Target golf practice should be saved for the second half of each practice session and for preround warm-up, given how difficult it is to turn off the conscious analytical mind when you step off the range and go to the first tee.

Practice to Play Golf Shots

Professionals never just beat balls or hit putts without complete focus, but that's how most amateurs practice. If you have trouble taking your practice game to the course, the first thing to do is to stop beating golf balls on the range military-style, which does not transfer well to playing golf shots on the course. Typical practice on the range does not simulate the requirements of a unique shot played on the course. Playing golf shots requires a shot-specific focus and use of imagination. You must think about club selection, lie of the ball, distance to the target, wind direction and intensity, and other environmental factors during shotmaking. Beating balls on the range often doesn't include this level of focus or creativity.

The best type of practice on the range is the type that simulates on-course play. Think about how you play a shot on the course. You must pick a target, calculate the distance for the shot, and select a club. You imagine and or feel the shot as you do your normal preshot routine. Focus and intensity on the course heightens because of this mental process, which is why your practice should mimic this process. Imagine you are hitting a familiar shot on the course. Pick a target each time you hit a shot. Imagine the ball flying to the target and practice going through your normal aim, alignment, and setup procedure, all part of making a shot. Take it a step further, and play 18 holes on the range by defining fairways and targets on the range that approximate the holes you will play on the course.

Final Thoughts

To help you transcend mechanics when you play, pay attention to the following points:

- Work on your swing only on the practice range or off-course. Don't practice your golf swing on the course.

- Groove a *repeatable* swing, not a perfect one. Develop a shot pattern you can rely on. Don't worry about how great your swing looks.

- Reduce swing cues to one thought, image, or feeling over the ball when you initiate the swing.

- Suspend your analytical mind by seeing the target in your mind as you execute the swing. If you are not a naturally visual player, focus instead on the feeling of the shot you want to hit.

- Play your usual shot and ball flight, not the one the course forces you to hit.

- Visualize and use your imagination to program yourself before each shot.

- Practice the right way by spending one-half of your time on target golf. See it, feel it, hit it. Low scores will be the result.

FOUR

Breaking New Ground with Ho-Hum Golf

Let it happen. Let the reins of the horse go and let him run as fast as he wants to run.

—GREG NORMAN (CAREER LOW: 63 IN THE 1996 MASTERS)

The professional tournaments you watch on TV every weekend represent a different class of golf from what amateurs play. It's more than just the superior physical ability of the tour professionals; you see the spectacle that results from television's need to sensationalize. Ho-hum golf is bad for television—but here's a secret: it's great for your performance.

Television shows us the best players in the world performing at the top of their games, and that's what makes the show exciting. Golf tournaments must entertain to keep the viewers tuned in. We generally see one superior shot after another, unless a player blows a crucial shot that causes him to lose the tournament. You certainly remember David Duval sinking a six-foot eagle putt on the 72nd hole of a tournament to shoot 59. You probably can recall the late Payne Stewart sinking a 20-footer for par on the final hole to win the 1999 U.S. Open. But you may not have seen Stewart play most of the first 71 holes of the tournament, which set up his heroic shot on the last hole. What you get is a distorted picture of how golf should be played—television golf seems to suggest that a player must be daring, bold, and courageous to win tournaments. We are left thinking, "Well, if Duval plays that way, that's the way I should try to play, too!"

Golf can be a very complex game, especially when we amateurs add to the problem. We begin by exposing ourselves to excess information on just the technical part of the game. To make matters worse, equipment manufacturers keep supplying us with an over-abundance of choices in everything from clubs and balls to training aids. Each time a club manufacturer introduces a new putter or high-tech club, you are compelled to trade up or let the competition get an edge over you.

One of your biggest challenges in breaking new ground by shooting lower and lower scores is to simplify a complex game that is getting more complex every year. Just a few years ago, your local club or driving range pro helped you with all phases of the game. But golf has become so specialized that we now have experts in every part of the game to help you improve. Specialization is great for the advancement of golf and player options, but for the individual player it can be very confusing. Here is a partial list of the areas in which you can now get specialized help:

- Equipment manufacturers offering individually fit clubs and gear
- Golf teachers with differing philosophies about how to learn, practice, and play golf
- Long game, short game, and putting specialists
- Sport psychologists who teach the mental side of golf
- Biomechanics experts who teach the kinesiology of the golf swing
- Physical therapists to help prevent and rehabilitate injuries
- Golf fitness specialists to help you get fit for golf
- Golf nutrition experts to recommend a diet for optimal performance

This multiplicity of sources and specialists is both positive and negative. The good news is you can go to a specialist who may be more qualified to help you with a particular area of the game. The bad news is that you now have more information, which can be confusing for many golfers.

As a consumer of all this information, how good a job do you do in filtering what you read and hear? Let's face it, golf is not an easy game to play or learn quickly. Just the physical abilities needed to hit a golf shot successfully are mind-boggling. You need good hand-eye coordination, balance, flexibility, timing, and other physical skills simply to make contact with the ball.

Besides needing a range of skills to hit a golf ball, you have to fight through the barrage of advice from different instructors, golf books, TV shows, and magazines. Golfers tend to consume and try everything they see, hear, or read. That's because most of them don't practice enough to finally trust their swings.

Also, golf challenges your mental abilities. Often the harder you try in golf, the worse you perform. Your intellect tells you to try harder and give more effort. If you fail, there is an urge to try even harder, but that doesn't help you shoot lower scores. To play well, you have to try less, which is very difficult for many amateurs to comprehend. Also very important is the discipline to focus on execution. Many amateurs don't know how to focus on execution and become easily distracted. Alas, confidence is an elusive asset for any golfer. It goes hand in hand with a certain emotional calmness needed to play well. Playing within your ability also means golfing with a cool head.

Don't forget that golf is a strategic game, a lot like chess. Besides formulating the best game plan to play the course, professionals pursue strategies that allow them to take advantage of their strengths on each hole. Planning each shot, however, is another way in which any player can make golf too complicated. For example, if you are getting ready to hit an iron shot from the fairway to a par-4 green, what factors must you consider? You pick a target, calculate the distance to the target, select a club, assess the lie of the ball (uphill, downhill, etc.), and determine the effects of the wind direction and air temperature. Don't forget about considering the landing area, where the pin is located on the green, how far you're hitting the 9-iron, and the trajectory and curve of the shot you want to hit.

Wow! That's a lot to think about for one shot, but the pros make these assessments and decisions with ease compared to their amateur counterparts. They have done it so many times that it becomes second nature.

You can further complicate your golf game by focusing too much on your opponents' games, worrying about beating them, or becoming overconcerned with what they think about you. Have you ever gotten into a driving contest with a playing partner and had it cost you the match? Many players take pride in outdriving their playing partners. It's another "game within the game" that golfers play, which I'll discuss later. But this is distracting, because trying to hit the longest drive doesn't always lead to better scoring.

In this chapter, you will learn two related lessons for shooting lower scores: (1) how to adopt a simplistic approach to golf, and (2) how to play within your abilities. You'll see how the pros have employed these skills to shoot the best rounds of their careers and perhaps adapt some of their tactics to your own play.

Finding the Flow with Simple Golf

Every player on the PGA, Senior PGA, and LPGA Tours strives to keep golf simple, which helps them play with less stress, less pressure, and more composure. What do I mean by keeping golf simple? I'm talking about how you go about your business on the golf course. This includes simplifying how you set your game plan and how you prepare to hit a shot or putt. We will even discuss the various ways that you interact with others on the golf course. A related lesson I discuss here is learning to play within your ability by not letting overconfidence and foolhardy instincts ruin your decision-making process. Playing within your ability simply means understanding your strengths, weaknesses, and limitations as a golfer. It also means using this information to play smarter so you can score your best.

Helen Alfredsson is a great example of a player who strives to make a complex game simple. Alfredsson scores her best when she plays within the bounds of the state of her game, whether that happens to be good or bad. At the 1994 U.S. Women's Open, Alfredsson shot a course-record 63 at Indianwood Golf & Country Club, the lowest round ever shot in Women's Open history. It was a breakthrough round for her mentally, because it was a difficult time in her career.

Most golf fans remember Alfredsson for blowing a lead in the final round of the 1993 U.S. Open at Crooked Stick. Even though she shot a 63 in the first round of the 1994 U.S. Open, she finished second because of poor play on the weekend. But shooting 63 gave her the boost of confidence she needed to win the Ping/Welch's Championship the very next week. Alfredsson admits she wasn't playing her best going into the 1994 Women's Open. Earlier in the year, she said she wasn't scoring well even though she was hitting the ball well, but Alfredsson knows that golf is unpredictable because performance can turn quickly in either direction. This conclusion was reinforced when she was playing in the Hennessey Cup in Germany two weeks before the 1994 U.S. Open. In one of the rounds, she struggled with her game. Her so-so play quickly turned around when she recorded an incredibly rare two-hole sequence of double eagle, eagle to finish, transforming a one-over-par round into a 69 and finishing in the top 10 that week. Your game can make a turn for the better in a flash, as Helen is quick to point out. "That is how it is with golf—you never know," she said.

The key to her fabulous 63 in the first round was her ability to pay attention to each shot and not become sidetracked by all the implications of playing well in a U.S. Open. "What I tried to do was on every shot just give it my fullest attention and try to do the best. I wasn't really thinking about where I was or what I had to do," she said—probably easier done in the first round of a major than in a final round. Alfredsson kept things simple and found that putting was the difference in the round: "It's a day where you just go on and do your business. You make a couple of putts and then you go on and you make more putts and all of a sudden you are six under. It is very hard to explain because it feels so simple, because nothing special happened. You simply hit good shots and make a few putts."

She shot three under par on the front side and then birdied holes 10, 12, and 14 to quickly get to six under par for the day. Some days when you start playing well it's not that easy. You make it harder by thinking too much about what you are playing for, what score you're shooting, or how big of a lead you may have. Not this day for Alfredsson, as she reflected: "Sometimes you are thinking too much ahead—and I knew there were a lot of tough holes coming in. I wasn't thinking, 'God, I am so many under now; I have to keep this.' I just tried to keep playing. And a lot of times when you do that, you actually keep making some birdies." And she did just that by making birdie at numbers 16 and 17 and finishing with a U.S. Women's Open record score of 63, eight under par.

> *I think it is important to just focus on your game and what you need to do and not think about what everybody else is doing.*
>
> —HELEN ALFREDSSON

The lesson here is that great players score their best when they make golf simple. They simplify the game by not changing their approach when playing in an important event. This skill is absolutely necessary to amateurs who want to simplify their own golf games. When you worry too much about winning a match or beating a rival, your game suffers because these thoughts distract you from focusing on execution. Golf also becomes too complicated when you think ahead and project your score. Focusing too much on score, your position in the tournament, or holes you have yet to play are just distractions that inhibit your ability to play golf in the moment.

Most players I've talked to say it's better to not pay attention to your score when going low. Focusing on score makes golf more complex and limits your ability to play in the now. Early in the round, it's easier to play without self-evaluation because you have many holes yet to play. It reminds me of a pitcher working on a no-hitter. The pitcher doesn't think about throwing a no-hitter in the first few innings, and no one talks about it. But later in the game, it becomes tougher to ignore the fact that a no-hitter is in progress. That's when the pitcher has to battle the excitement and distractions of throwing a perfect game.

The same is true when shooting a low round of golf. As you get closer to the last hole, it's harder to ignore the possibility of shooting a best score ever. It is now more important than ever to not get too excited about shooting a good round and stay focused on your game. You have enough distractions to contend with. You don't want to make it more difficult by stressing out about your potential score. Alfredsson agrees that it's best not to pay attention to score, watch the leader board, or think about your position in the tournament: "A lot of times when you are playing well, you start seeing too much. Then, coming into the last few holes, you have a tendency of thinking about how many under you are. It's great when you do play well, but you just go on and focus. I wasn't thinking I was eight under, but it's not always like that when you are shooting a really good score. You don't even know what you are doing sometimes. It wasn't that hard—that is how you feel when you are shooting eight under. Why can't I do this every day?" Every day is a different day in golf.

If you try too hard to shoot a low score, you make golf more complicated. The harder you try in golf, the worse your performance. When you try hard, the mind is in overtime working out all the little details and making sure you have not forgotten something. The best option when putting, for example, is to rely on imagination and feel. "A lot of people think too many things. If you can stand up and see the ball roll in the hole time after time, you are creating a sort of confidence," Alfredsson said.

Golf is definitely played between the ears, but the brain can get clogged with details when you try too hard mentally. Accounting for every variable that will affect a shot causes information overload. In putting, for example, the best putters in the world rely on their vision, imagination, and experience. You can't reduce putting to a formula—it isn't like the problems you solved in high school physics or geometry. The body cannot stroke a putt freely while the mind is calculating the severity of slope, direction of grain, speed of the green, wind strengths and direction, spike marks on your line, and how these factors together will come into play. Your body will freeze up, because it doesn't know how to react to all the input from the mind.

LPGA star Wendy Ward is another player who strives to simplify her golf game. She used this philosophy in 1997 to shoot an LPGA all-time 72-hole scoring record with a total of 265 (−23) during the Fieldcrest Cannon Classic. The week before her record performance, she missed the cut because of poor putting. After working with her instructor, she came back with a new approach, which was to have more fun on the course and not become so absorbed in the "have-to" attitude about making putts. Focusing too much on results also makes golf more complicated than needed, as Ward says: "I think you can get overconcerned with results. Enjoy the process; enjoy the opportunity to play. That one week I committed to having fun, I enjoyed the time being out there; each shot, each hole, I made the most of every moment and stayed out of my way." Wendy is able to carry this outlook beyond the golf course. "It's kind of the way I live my life—each day is a new day, a new opportunity. What I did the previous day is not in my mind."

For Ward, simplicity also means quieting the mind so she can do her job better. Everyone has an inner voice, what psychologists call "self-talk." I'm sure you have had days when your inner voice is rambling and it's hard to quiet that voice. It happens when you have too much on your mind, either worries about other things in your life or by overthinking your game. "Sometimes our minds get where the voice is just talking and buzzing in our ear instead of being just quiet. And that week, I had . . . a quiet mind. Give me the information I need for this shot, and let me execute—no indecision over the ball," Ward said.

Ward noticed a comforting rhythm with her game as she prepared for each shot. Rhythm is good in golf. Doing the same things to prepare for every shot and sticking to the basics of a preshot routine may sound boring, but for most professionals it is the standard recipe for low-scoring golf. "It started to become repetitious, because I was seeing shots go to the hole before I hit them," explained Ward, "and then it was just a matter of making the swing. All of a sudden, I am watching the shot I just saw two seconds ago in my mind. That's fun—I never before experienced that," she said. If you try something new on every shot, a different image, thought, or swing cue, it's more difficult to play consistently. I realize it's hard not to change what you do on the next shot after hitting the last one in the woods. "That didn't work. I guess I'll try something different this time," you say to yourself as you begin to play the next shot. It's really a mistake. Don't let poor results make you change your approach from shot to shot.

Keys to Simplifying Your Game

I've discussed how the pros strive for simplicity, which helps them record low rounds. The same tenets hold true for you, too. The ability to stay composed, leave your worries at home, not be distracted by other players, and simplify your shotmaking are all skills that will help you score a breakthrough round. Let's explore each of these.

Cool and Collected Golf

If you want to model your demeanor after another player, Fred Couples is an ideal choice. He keeps his emotions on an even keel. He never gets too excited after making a birdie or eagle; nor does he get upset after making a bogey or double bogey—at least that's the way it appears from an observer's perspective. If you let your emotions get out of control, this interferes with the ability to make rational decisions. When was the last time you hit a good drive after making a stupid double bogey on the previous hole and getting upset with yourself? You can't carry your anger or frustration to the next tee. If you do, the anger will make you try for the big drive, swing too fast, or you'll just lose interest temporarily in your game (players refer to this as "when the bubble bursts," when they feel deflated and lose intensity). It's much easier to hit your next shot if you can stay in control and refocus on what you need to do.

Take Your Golf Bag, Not Your Baggage

Good golfers know they have to play golf with a mind free of life's problems. Even the professionals struggle with their games when they bring life's worries to the golf course. When playing golf, your role must switch to golfer. Just lacing up your golf shoes and pulling the golf bag over your shoulder should signal it's time to switch roles and leave your real-life responsibilities off the course until you finish. One reason people engage in sports is to be relieved for a short while of the doldrums or problems of life—the "escape theory" of sport participation. Although your job or home life is more important than golf, it's best for your game and mental health to suspend those worries about work or home life while playing golf. You can't address these worries until you get off the course, anyway. So when it's time to play golf, immerse yourself in the role of golfer.

Focus on Your Game

Professional golfers are well aware of the need to pay attention to their own games and not be influenced by the agenda of their playing partners. Don't allow your playing partners' games to distract you. I'm not just talking about watching their golf game. I'm also referring to how playing partners play games within the game. Don't get sucked into the who-can-hit-the-longest-tee-shot game, for example. Psych-outs is another game some players may use to distract you. Greg Norman, for example, was a master at this. He would stand on the tee box and take practice swings with his driver to influence his playing partners' club selection. After they hit, he would put the driver in the bag and pull out an iron to hit off the tee, which was his plan all along. Some golfers play extra slowly when you want to keep a brisk pace; others rush all over the course while you are trying to slow things down and prepare for a shot.

Don't Overanalyze

The adage "overanalysis leads to paralysis" is very true in golf. One of the inherent difficulties of golf for some players is the amount of time they have to prepare for shots. In reality, this is both an advantage and an obstacle to overcome. The advantage is that you don't have to hit a shot until you are fully ready. The problem is that this extra time can be misused. When you use that time to overanalyze every shot and putt, the brain gets clogged and sends poor signals to the body. The mind can process only a certain amount of information at one time.

A good example of this is overreading greens. You look at your putt from behind the ball and see the putt as right edge. Then you go to the other side of the hole and see it as a straight putt. After an internal debate, you circle around the putt another time to decide how much the grain will affect the putt. So far, you are doing what any golfer would do, but when you start to introduce several other factors that may affect your read, such as wind, outcome of last putt, and so on, the mind becomes bogged down in details. Great putters, such as Ben Crenshaw, relax and let their imagination account for all the variables. Whatever line to the hole Crenshaw sees initially he uses. He doesn't second-guess himself as more and more information is introduced.

Quiet the Mind

Earlier I talked about how a quiet mind is necessary to get into the flow and become immersed in execution. How do you quiet the mind? First, don't ruminate about past shots or holes and let them obstruct your thinking. Be totally focused on the shot you have now, not the one you had 10 minutes ago. Meditation experts teach their students to silently repeat a mantra (a word with no meaning) to quiet the mind. If other thoughts come to mind, you're instructed to let them pass and focus back on the mantra. I don't expect you to meditate on the course, but you can focus attention on your breathing just before you prepare for a shot. If other thoughts come to mind, let them pass and refocus on the rhythm of your breathing. You can use a simple golf-specific "mantra" to quiet the mind and focus on the basics of your preshot routine, such as "see it, feel it, and do it" or "plan, rehearse, and execute."

Enjoyment Should Be a Primary Goal

What's the most important goal when you play golf? Is it to win a match? Shoot the lowest score possible? Win a few dollars from a best friend? Enjoy the company of friends? Or have the most fun possible? If you said have fun, give yourself 10 bonus points. Golf becomes more complicated when you place too much importance on a personal agenda, such as beating your best friend in a small wager. I'm not against betting on the golf course, but it can become a distraction when it becomes more important to win the bet than to have fun. You'll win if you are focused on playing each shot to the best of your ability and having fun. Instead of worrying about how to beat your friend, try to have fun with her seriousness.

Playing Ho-Hum Golf

Playing your best golf is not about playing the heroic or sensational golf that television portrays. There is great fun and excitement to shooting a good round of golf, but it usually doesn't take daring or sensational play to do it. Both Ernie Els and Steve Jones would attest to this. They are able to go low often because each knows when to play aggressively and when to play conservatively. They know exactly what their capabilities are. Many amateur golfers are not in tune with what shots they can and cannot successfully execute on the golf course. Many amateurs subscribe to a "pedal to the metal" mind-set that doesn't take into account their true ability level or the consequences of going for broke.

Watch David Duval or Fred Couples play golf. They both look calm, as though their round is a walk in the park. They strive for ho-hum golf. "Ho-hum golf" is used to describe golf that is boring but productive. And by *boring*—which is generally a negative word—most players are referring to an inner calmness that is quite wonderful to experience. The goal is to hit fairways and greens, two-putt for par, and occasionally make a putt for birdie. And if they get hot with the putter, they can shoot low.

One trait that separates pros from you, the amateur, is their ability to use boring golf to help them play good golf. Most amateur golfers who want to score low are committed to hitting John Daly–like drives, trying for every green in two no matter the cost, sinking every chip, and putting with the boldness of Tiger Woods.

It's an "I-can-do-it-approach"—and a frivolous one, at that. The need for instant gratification (to make a heroic shot) pushes golfers to play with little concern for the consequences of a missed shot.

You are probably asking yourself, "Do I really want to play boring golf?" That depends. If you live for the thrill that going for broke gives you when you try to hit a driver over the corner of a dogleg, then you hate to play a boring style of golf. But if you want to shoot low scores and make a breakthrough, a boring style of golf is the route. Ho-hum or boring golf has such a negative tone to it. Shouldn't golf be exciting to play? I think a better term to use is "sensible golf," which is playing golf under control and within the limits of your ability and skills. Let's discuss some ideas for playing sensible golf.

Know Your Limitations

Understanding just what shots you are capable of hitting successfully is the most important principle for playing within your abilities. Pride often tells you to hit that 3-iron over the water to reach the green—after all, you hit one or two 3-iron shots solidly in warm-up, right? What's the likelihood of your hitting a good clean shot successfully over the water? You see pros do it all the time on television. Aren't you supposed to go for it? No, you are supposed to play the high-percentage shot that helps you score your best. In Chapter 9, I'll detail how to use good course management to score better.

Macho Is for Boxing, Not for Golf

Many male amateur golfers played football, hockey, and other contact sports in Little League, high school, or college before taking up golf. These sports encourage the participants to play aggressively and dominate the opponent. Coaches and other teammates reinforce macho, aggressive behavior. I know this because I played football, hockey, and lacrosse in high school and lacrosse in college. But golfers need a mind-set different from that of athletes in contact sports, especially football. Golf demands discipline, control, and finesse.

Hitting the biggest drive in the foursome may be satisfying to you, but hitting the longest drive doesn't always win golf matches. Ho-hum golf is about playing finesse golf, not power golf. Ho-hum golf, for example, suggests you use any club necessary to get your ball in the fairway so you can set up your next shot.

Chip Beck's 59: A Childhood Premonition

As a child, Chip Beck dreamed that it could happen—that someday he would shoot a 59 on the PGA Tour. He claims he will never forget his first lesson in low scoring: watching his childhood teaching pro, Tony Evans, shoot 60 with pars on the last two holes. Seeing Tony shoot 60 gave Beck the inspiration and hope that someday it would be possible to shoot 59 on the PGA Tour. During the third round of the 1991 Las Vegas Invitational, Beck realized his dream. Making 13 birdies and no bogeys at Sunrise Golf Club, Beck became only the second player to shoot 59 on the PGA Tour.

Chip's goal was to not think about shooting 59 until he found himself in the middle of a hot round with a legitimate chance to actually do it. After shooting 29 on the front side, Beck knew he had a chance and started to think about shooting 59. A volunteer told him he had the lowest score on the front side by three or four shots, with the easy side coming up. When he had three holes remaining, Beck asked the volunteer if the million-dollar bonus offered by Hilton Hotels for shooting 59 was still in effect. The volunteer told him it was. "I said, 'Great!' It gave me more incentive to shoot 59," Beck recalled.

At 10 under par with three holes remaining, Beck's goal was to give himself chances to make birdies on the last three holes. After making birdie on 16, he had to hit a great approach shot on 17 just to have a chance at making birdie. It was a tricky pin on 17 that required him to bounce a shot from the front fringe into the pin. He hit it perfectly and drained a 10-footer to go to

12 under par. He struggled to stay focused on 18. "I was thinking, 'Gosh, it's getting harder to hit the fairway.' I was trying not to think about shooting 59 too much—just see my line and hit my target, and I did." After going back and forth between an 8- and 7-iron, he decided to hit the 8-iron, the club he thought would give him the best chance to hole the shot.

He set up to the ball and made a swing. "When I hit it, I knew it came out perfect, just as I had visualized it: the height, the spin, everything. And so I thought it was going to be really close. I actually thought it was a foot from the hole. When I got up there it was a three-foot downhill putt—that's kind of a challenging putt," said Beck.

He went to the side of the green and tried to relax and gather his thoughts. He didn't want to be thinking over the putt. He was going to stay as steady as possible, give it his best shot, and go through his routine. Even with two spike marks right on his line, he didn't panic. He could see the ball just missing the spike marks and catching the hole. "I visualized the ball going in no matter what, and it did," Beck said. He finished in a tie for second but landed in elite company as only the second person to shoot 59 in an official PGA Tour event.

Play Sensible Golf

Besides understanding your limitations as a golfer and playing with finesse, ho-hum golf is simply about playing smart. By definition, ho-hum golf is a strategy that uses any means to help you hit the fairway, hit the green, and two-putt or one-putt on every hole. It's not a protective or overconservative style of golf. If you play a protective style of golf, you try to avoid making mistakes such as missing greens and staying away from water hazards—almost as if you are scared to make mistakes.

Ho-hum golf is not about playing scared. When playing ho-hum golf, you use a smart game plan to keep the ball in play for 18 holes and play high-percentage shots. It means using sound course management. Professionals do this much better than amateurs because of their experience, but also because they know it's the only way to shoot the best score any day. Once in a while, you may shoot a low score by employing an aggressive, I-can-hit-any-shot style of play, but most often this approach will cause your scores to soar.

Final Thoughts

Golf, although a complex game, needs to be played with simplicity. When you worry too much about beating a rival or hitting perfect shots, or when you bring other life worries into golf, your performance suffers because it's harder to just focus on execution. The best golfers know they need to maintain a level head and keep their emotions on an even keel. You should strive to adopt a mentality of playing ho-hum golf. Shooting low scores is about hitting fairways, greens, and two-putting for par. Don't get sucked away from a focus on your game plan and into playing macho games within the game.

Shooting Low with a Home-Course "Disadvantage"

Playing in front of my family and hometown kept me pretty
focused, and the fact that I did have a chance to win the
tournament was the key to going low.

—MEG MALLON (CAREER LOW: 62)

Michael Jordan, John Elway, and Tiger Woods all reached the pinnacles of their respective fields in large part due to their ability "to finish off a game." When under the gun, these great athletes thrive. They each want to take the last shot, make the game-winning pass, and sink that birdie putt on the last hole to win. They live for the moment of most intense competition, to thrill the fans and experience the excitement of winning. Great athletes excel when the fans are behind them and victory is nearby. They thrive on a home-court, home-field, or home-course advantage. Meanwhile, less experienced athletes crumble under the pressure and expectations of playing at home.

How do great athletes excel with the pressure of everyone they care about watching and urging them on, while other athletes cripple themselves with fear of failure and embarrassment in the same situation? It has a lot to do with experience, having been in that situation a hundred times before. But players' personalities and how they perceive the challenges and therefore how they prepare themselves must also be taken into account. Great golfers, such as Tiger

Woods, raise their performance to a higher level when playing in front of hometown fans and family. The added incentive, adrenaline high, and excitement stoke their competitive fires, helping them peak their focus and go deeper into the zone. They don't ever choke themselves with fears of what others will think if they screw up and how they will face family and friends if they lose.

Let's relate this phenomenon to the most stressful situation an amateur golfer will typically face: anxiety about the first tee shot. The so-called first-tee jitters pose a classic challenge. To dramatize this point, I will tell you about my golfing friend, Sandy. The last time I played golf with Sandy, he topped the ball off the first tee. It didn't shock me or make me think any differently of him, but he was so embarrassed his face turned cherry red. By nature, Sandy is self-conscious. He cares a lot about what other people think of him. The root of self-consciousness lies in social evaluation theory, which maintains that a person's behavior is influenced to some degree by how other people evaluate him. This is true of everyone, but it's a matter of degree. The more you care about how others perceive you, the more likely you are to change your behavior to gain others' approval.

Golf provides all of us with multiple chances to embarrass ourselves, but a player like Sandy has a personality that makes him particularly self-conscious on the links. First, he doesn't want to embarrass himself with a bad tee shot. This would make him look like a real hacker, and that's the last label he wants. Second, he needs to earn his friends' respect and desperately wants the other players in the group to like him. He hopes golf can be an avenue for this purpose. Third, he doesn't want to discourage his partner—in this case me, because we are playing together in a two-man better-ball tournament at the club. He worries that his poor shot will upset me and make me think less of him. Last, he knows other people are watching him tee off—including the club pro, from whom he has been taking lessons. Sandy desperately wants Ed to think all the lessons are paying off. Knowing all this background information about Sandy, I am sure you can understand why he topped his first tee shot.

Sandy, like many other amateur golfers, can't score to his potential primarily because of a few "mental traps" he gets caught in.

These traps generally are of three types: (1) social evaluation and general self-consciousness, (2) stage fright or fear of being the center of attention, and (3) negative group dynamics, meaning the willingness to let others in the group affect one's performance. All three of these phenomena can add up to what I term a "home-course disadvantage." Playing at your home course with friends whose approval you desire puts you at a disadvantage, because you worry too much about how others see you and how they judge you. These concerns keep you from performing up to your potential. In this chapter, I'll describe how the pros use the emotions from their fans to play better, what the most common mental traps look like and feel like, and how to avoid them.

Notah Begay's 59: When You're Hot, Run the Tables

Notah Begay, a half-Navajo and half-Pueblo Indian, was raised on a reservation in Albuquerque, New Mexico. He was the first Nike Tour player ever to shoot 59, and the third in PGA Tour history. Begay's round consisted of nine birdies, two eagles, and no bogeys. Starting on the back nine, the round started slowly with just one birdie on the first five, but Begay made a late charge by recording birdies on three of the last four holes. After a four-under-par 32 on the first nine, the real fireworks began. Notah shot a record-tying nine-under-par 27 on the back.

On his back nine, he started with a bang—eagle, birdie, eagle on the first three holes. He holed a wedge on the par-4 first hole and made a hole-in-one on the 175-yard third. Begay also birdied holes five and six to get to 11 under par for the round. After parring hole number seven, he sank a 30-foot birdie putt at eight. He had to make an eight-foot birdie putt at number nine to shoot 59. Standing behind the putt, he said to himself, "This is what you practice for; this is what you work for. Let's go get a piece of history."

Begay thinks that most pro golfers are technically capable of shooting 59. "But that's not the hard part," said Begay. The problem starts when players "get in their own way." "It's the mental struggle to get out of your own way and let things happen. You don't get many days like that in your life, so when it does happen, you just acknowledge it and go with the flow," said Begay.

Although he etched his name in the golf books with a 59, he wasn't happy with his performance on the weekend. Begay shot a pair of 74s Saturday and Sunday to finish tied for sixth. It was his best finish on the Nike Tour up to that date, but more important, it gave him the spark he needed to play well the rest of the year. He qualified for the PGA Tour by finishing 10th on the 1998 Nike Tour.

The Cheerleading Effect

Professional golfers have a distinct advantage when they play a tournament at their home course. They have a special familiarity with the course, because they play it and practice on it when they aren't out on tour. They develop a big advantage on the greens, for example, by learning every break and undulation. When they play a tournament on this course, they gain the advantage of being able to stay at home, live and eat with family, and take the short drive to the course. No plane trips, no searching for restaurants to eat at, no unfamiliar hotels.

You, too, are privy to home-course knowledge at your home course or local club. For some golfers, however, there is also undue pressure to play well at home. That goes for the pros, too. If Steve Jones plays in the Phoenix Open in Scottsdale, he knows a lot of hometown fans will come out to watch him play. Friends and family also join in the fanfare. Of course, Jones wants to play well for all of them. Isn't he supposed to play well at the TPC of Scottsdale, where he practices all the time? Ah yes, another expectation. But despite these pressures, Jones plays well in Phoenix. The home-course advantages somehow outweigh the pressures to play well. Could Jones be using the pressure as motivation to play better? Now, that's a possibility.

That is, in fact, what Jones did when he wowed his fans during the 1997 Phoenix Open, setting a 72-hole PGA Tour scoring record and winning by 11 shots over Jesper Parnevik. Jones has won eight times on the PGA Tour, including the 1996 U.S. Open, so he has experience. But Jones is by nature a performer and an entertainer on the golf course. Unlike my friend Sandy, he enjoys playing to the crowds, especially his hometown fans in Phoenix. At the Phoenix Open that year, he shot rounds of 62, 65, 65, and 67. His 16-under cumulative score of 126 for the first two rounds tied the PGA record for best 36 holes starting a tournament. He needed only 96 putts for the week, an average of 24 putts per round, which is phenomenal.

Jones milks the home-course advantage for everything it's worth. Instead of crumbling under the pressure to perform at home, he thrives on the cheerleading of his friends and fans pulling for him. Jones said, "I had about 150 friends at Phoenix, people I knew really well, and I think that helps. It's like a home-court advantage, and I always love playing at Phoenix for that reason. You get momentum going, and they are urging you on like cheerleaders. It feeds the momentum." If you have never seen the fans at the Phoenix Open, trust me, they can get vocal. I watched Jones when he played in contention at Phoenix in 1998. His fans and friends live and die with every shot he takes. And Jones loves to ham it up for them.

Jones flourishes at Phoenix with the help of his cheerleaders. He electrifies his fans, and vice versa. He and his followers feed off each other—the more electricity, the better he focuses and the sharper his game gets. "When I have a little momentum and I get a little emotional, I think it helps me. I think that's part of what Tiger feeds on, because he is very emotional and he feeds on that. A lot of players do the same, including Nicklaus and Palmer. They played with emotion," Jones said. Emotion, yes, but let me qualify Jones's comment by saying the *right kind* of emotion.

The type of emotion Jones refers to is very positive. It's instrumental in helping him fully concentrate. The extra intensity he gets from wanting to play well for his fans and friends is channeled into his emotions to help him get to an optimal level of concentration. Of course, negative emotions can ruin a round. The fear of losing the tournament with a big lead, the anxiety of playing with a lead, and the frustration that comes after making a bogey are the killers of a round.

In thriving on his home turf, Steve Jones is not alone. I can give you many other examples of players who love the scrutiny and challenges of playing at home. Meg Mallon is one who comes quickly to mind. She shot a career-low 62 in the first round of the 1998 Myrtle Beach Classic, a tournament in which she went on to finish second. Her 10-under-par round tied the LPGA 18-hole scoring record. One advantage was that she knew the course well and had past success there. Another advantage was that a legion of friends and family watched her play that week, which transported her out of the normal lonely grind of golf into a sporting event with cheering fans. "The whole crowd was into it. It was like being a part of a sporting event like a football game, where people were cheering and rooting for you. There was a lot of excitement that day," Mallon reflected.

> *[Today was] exciting because I had big gallery and they make noise. I play better because there are many people watching. I feel more excited when many people are there. It makes me want to show them great shots.*
>
> —SE RI PAK, REFLECTING ON HER CAREER-LOW 61

Mallon, like Jones, loves the intensity that comes with playing in front of friends. She had much better concentration that week because of the cheerleading effect and because she had a chance to win the tournament. "I like playing in front of others, because it does help me be more focused, less distracted, stick more to the task at hand, and get really involved in my golf game and just play," she said. What a great definition of concentration! The best golfers go deeper into a zone of concentration when they are faced with competitive pressures. In this case, she used the fanfare and emotion of winning to go low.

Mallon rejects the idea that the presence of others ought to make her nervous. She is not playing to impress her friends; instead her goal is for everyone, including herself, to have fun. Mallon strives to keep her game in perspective and to play for the right reasons. "I like having that atmosphere. It's fun, because I'm enjoying playing well and they are enjoying themselves watching me play well. I want my fans to enjoy themselves, but I don't feel an overwhelming sense of having to perform well in front of other people. I have golf in perspective, where it's not a burden to play great golf. So it's important to me to play well because I work hard and I want to do the right things, but I also understand how difficult the game is and that I can't pressure myself," she said.

Tiger Woods is another pro who loves to play close to home. Woods shot a 10-under-par 62 in the third round of the 1999 Buick Invitational, his first 62 as a pro and a course record at Torrey Pines South. Torrey Pines is a course Woods knows well from junior golf because he won his sixth Optimist Junior World Golf Championship at Torrey Pines South at the age of 15 in 1991. "I do have some good vibes here; I always have. I've always liked playing here in San Diego—actually Southern California, period. This is where I grew up," Woods said. He, too, loves the support of friends and hometown fans. "You can't really say enough how much that really affects you—to see people you know out there supporting you. You don't get to see it every week as you travel all over the world. Most of the time you're alone, you and your caddie," Woods said.

The Mental Traps of Playing at Home

Tiger Woods, Steve Jones, and Meg Mallon are examples of players who have shot career-low rounds playing on familiar ground. They feed off the emotions of playing at home, which heightens their intensity and helps them become more immersed in their golf. In most instances, the average golfer doesn't play in front of spectators. But we do play with other people, and sometimes to impress other people. If you play for others or alter your behavior to accommodate your friends or competitors, you are falling into a home-course disadvantage, letting the distractions of playing at home block you from getting into the flow of concentrating on the task at hand. Let's identify the major mental traps you may fall prey to on the course.

Need for Approval

Sandy, you recall, is our example of a player who has a counterproductive need for approval. Everyone has a preference to be liked and get approval from friends and family, but with some people it's a dire need. The root of this problem is Sandy's low self-esteem. People with low self-esteem try to use the approval of others to bolster their own self-esteem. Sandy is convinced he must perform well to gain approval from others, which places undue pressure on his game. Instead of thinking about hitting a good tee shot, he's worried about others' perception of him if he messes up.

Fear of Embarrassment

No one likes to hit a bad shot and embarrass himself or herself, but some people just don't care what others think about them. The fear of embarrassment turns out to be worse than the emotion of being embarrassed itself. And what a waste of emotional energy! Your anxiety about hitting a bad shot—a problem that has not even happened yet—will always pose a major distraction to focusing on executing a good shot. The saying "We have nothing to fear but fear itself" holds true for you in this instance.

Stage Fright

Stage fright is a fear related to being the center of attention. This is the feeling Sandy had when everyone was watching him on the first tee. All eyes were on him—his pro, his playing partners, and the next group waiting to tee off. Stage fright intensifies our feelings of embarrassment, because the cost of hitting a bad shot or messing up a good round is greater when other people are watching. Many people literally freeze up and can't perform in this state. When shooting a low round, you often become the center of attention in the group, and this can be very distracting as you try to play one shot at a time, especially when playing partners remind you that you are in the process of shooting your lowest round ever.

Psych-Outs

Psych-outs occur when another person tries to upset your rhythm by distracting you mentally so he or she can get the upper hand. Psych-outs come in many different forms. The first and most common is "concentration derailment." This is a subtle form of psych-out that occurs, for example, when your playing partner purposely walks in your putting line while you putt or jingles pocket coins while you swing. Another psych-out is the "confidence stab," which is a more direct form of psych-out than concentration derailment. Here, a player might try to upset you with a comment such as "You can't make a putt to save your life." A third category is "overanalysis digs," where a playing partner might point out something in your swing or your putting stroke to make you overthink, such as "Wow, your backswing looks smoother today. What is your swing cue?" A fourth type of psych-out is "strategy indecision," where a player tries to get you to second-guess your strategy on a hole or shot, asking, "Don't you think driver is too much on this hole?" One other type of psych-out is "try-harder seduction," where your playing partner says something to get you angry and make you try harder to beat him.

Betting

Betting can become a mental trap for many players if they let the anxiety of losing a bet affect their games. For some players, betting is an asset because it gives them an added incentive to play better, thereby notching up their concentration a level or two. I don't recommend that you bet for this reason, because you should be able to concentrate fully without this added incentive. But betting can turn into a form of psych-out when a playing partner keeps increasing the stakes in the hopes of making you too anxious about "the money on the table" to perform well, or perhaps to make you try harder to win. If you are playing the best round of your life, you are probably ahead in any bet you may have made, but it still can distract you from finishing off the round.

Rivalry

Rivalry with another player at your club or hometown can have a positive effect on your motivation to improve, practice more, and do everything you can to beat your opposition. But it's not usually helpful when playing a round against your archrival unless you use the rivalry to motivate you to play better. If you take it deep one day against your rival, a friendly rivalry can turn into a fierce dogfight. If you are trying to shoot the best round ever, it's usually not helpful to be playing against someone who wants to beat you badly. He or she may begin to use psych-outs to derail your concentration.

Negative Group Undercurrents

If you are playing well, it's easier to continue to play well when other players in your group are also playing well—you are pulled along in a group current of good play. There is a vicarious reinforcement effect—the feeling that "if she can do it, so can I." Likewise, it can be very distracting to have another golfer in the group who is playing very poorly. It's hard to keep your focus, especially when this player is throwing tantrums after every bad shot. You can't help but notice this player's desperation, which can tow you under and throw you off your rhythm.

Calming Your Fears

So far I have talked about how professionals use the excitement of fans and friends to help them go deeper into a zone and play better when playing at home. But the opposite is true for amateurs. You are disadvantaged when playing at your home club, not because you have thousands of people watching you play, but because of negative group interaction, fear of embarrassment, and your own social self-consciousness. Let's discuss how you can play better by shedding the fears of social evaluation and the negative influence of the group.

Who Really Cares?

One of the biggest handcuffs you can play with is the need for approval. It tells me that you lack self-esteem and try to gain it from others. What if you really didn't care about what others thought of you or your game? That tells me that you believe in yourself and won't let others influence how you feel. What if I told you that your friends really don't make judgments about you based on how well you play? They certainly shouldn't, not if they are your true friends. What do you think about your best friend when he tops his tee shot or plays a poor round? No big deal, right? So why don't you turn it around and look at your game the same way? The bottom line is you can't be self-conscious and care about what others think about you.

If a pro ever thought about what judgments the gallery were making about him, he would never finish the round. The presence of other people is not a distraction for the pros; rather, it's helpful for many seasoned players. They channel the energy from performing center stage positively to help them focus more on golf. I can see how a brain surgeon could feel pressure from the family members of his patient. After all, the patient's life is in his hands, and if something goes wrong, he has to deal with the patient's family. But still, the surgeon knows pressure is counterproductive to doing his job well. So he either ignores the pressure or uses it to focus intensely on the immediate task.

Self-Forgetfulness and the Flow of Golf

We've learned that two golfers in the same situation can react in two different ways. One player, who loves the attention of playing in the club championship, uses it to help him go deeper into a bubble of concentration and thus plays well. The other player in the same situation, who's afraid to fail and embarrass himself if he blows the match, cannot get focused and thus plays poorly. What is it that differentiates these players mentally? Is it personality, emotions, self-esteem, or confidence? It's probably a combination of all four. I can say that one of these players is able to get into flow—into that state of total immersion in the task. Ask yourself: with all the entanglements of betting, psych-outs, rivalry, and other negative group influences, can I reasonably expect to get into the flow of the round?

Flow happens when you are in a state of self-forgetfulness, which is the opposite of worry about what others think about you and your game. When in this flow, you are totally absorbed in the immediate shot without attaching any consequences to it. In flow, you are in total control of your performance, instinctively reacting to the environment. You are unconcerned about how you are doing; it's the *doing* that is most important. You do it for the pure pleasure that it gives you, without attaching rewards or negative consequences to the outcome.

How does one get into the flow? The first requirement to getting into the flow is that you have clear goals and get specific feedback about how you are doing. Sport itself provides clear goals and outcomes. In golf, the goal is to hit your shot at the target, and you learn quickly just how well you did after hitting the shot. This goal-feedback relationship helps to hold your concentration on execution, thereby pushing out unrelated "static." The second requirement to flow is to become immersed in the task. Once locked into the task, the mind releases self-induced pressures and day-to-day preoccupations. The third requirement to flow relates to your perception of the difficulty of the task. If you perceive that your skills are not equal to the challenges of the task (your opponent is much better than you, or you don't have the skill to hit the shot, for example), you become anxious, which interrupts flow. Likewise, when you perceive the challenge to be too low for your skill level, boredom interrupts flow.

So to get into the flow, you need to feel that your skills match up well with the challenge. But the task must be challenging enough to help you get excited about achieving the goal. This means that a higher demand than usual—but a demand that is still within your capabilities—will be optimal for flow. Herein lies the reason why many pros are able to get into the flow and play better in the presence of others. The added incentive to perform well in the presence of others forces them to focus more intensely and go deeper into the zone—whereas amateurs become overwhelmed and perceive the challenge as excessive, which causes anxiety and a loss of focus.

Final Thoughts

Once again, we circle back to the importance of confidence in golf. As your confidence grows, so does your estimation of the challenges you can conquer. For example, if you feel confident that you can hit a good first tee shot, you don't become anxious about the outcome and thus immerse yourself in the task. Based on what we know about athletes performing well when in flow, you should strive to do three simple assignments:

1. Have clear goals of what you want to accomplish (i.e., hit the ball in the fairway to a specific target).

2. Become immersed in the ingredients of the task that help you achieve that goal by picking a target, seeing the ball go there, and paying attention to setup and execution.

3. Be confident that you can achieve that task by believing your skills are good enough to hit the ball in the fairway without attaching any consequences to that belief.

In this involved state, the mind is locked into completing the challenge. Self-consciousness and fears about what others think disappear. The mind works more efficiently in this state, and thus your performance feels effortless. You are concentrating, but you don't have to force yourself to do so. You want to complete the task above all else, with no emotional static or negative outcomes attached. If you perceive the challenge to be too great and worry about the consequences of hitting the errant shot, what others will think, or losing the match, anxiety and fear block you from maintaining a task-specific focus.

Turn your home-course disadvantage into a home-course advantage. The ability to use the social pressures to help you become immersed in the task is your assignment. This holds true when you feel pressure to take a low round in progress to the clubhouse. Instead of worrying about feeling embarrassed about what others will think if you blow a great round, use that challenge to help you go deeper into the flow.

SIX

Taking It All the Way to the Clubhouse

If you think about what score you're shooting, then you end up protecting instead of concentrating on the shot at hand.

—TAMMY GREEN (CAREER LOW: 63)

What makes great athletes like Michael Jordan able to perform in pressure situations? Confidence? Personal triumph? When Jordan takes the ball, the opposing team is prepared, his team depends on him to win, and his fans watch in anticipation. But Jordan knows that scoring the winning shot is not just about winning a ball game. He realizes it is about commanding his emotions and relishing the excitement of the moment. He loves the inner battle and thrives under the pressure. Like many other great athletes, Jordan has learned to thrive under pressure when other athletes might choke in the same situation.

To shoot your lowest round ever, you must love the pressure to make a par on the last hole. You have the physical skills to do it, but can you make a scoring breakthrough by overcoming the psychological battle? You were introduced to the concept of comfort zones and how they shape your behavior in Chapter 1.

Comfort zones are expectations you have about what you're capable of shooting on any given day. You form expectations based on your experience and previous golf scores. When you are playing better than expected, a comfort zone becomes self-defeating, because it limits and prevents you from playing golf in the *now*.

In Chapter 1, you learned how to identify and eradicate self-limiting beliefs that cause you to mentally sabotage your success. In this chapter, you will learn the central lesson of how to continue to play with a "lead" and score your best. You will also learn how pro golfers overcome comfort zones to go on to shoot career-low rounds.

Two players with similar golf skills who contend differently with comfort zones will be contrasted to highlight the defeatist role of playing in a comfort zone: Tina, a 13-handicap who is limited by a comfort zone, and Sally, a 10-handicap who has learned how to overcome the limitations of a comfort zone.

On the front nine, Tina was playing great, shooting a 39. Her biggest mental challenge on the back nine would be to continue to play well. In the past, if she shot a 40 or less on the front, she would get too anxious about breaking 80. Tina's first mistake was focusing too much on her score. Because she was focused on score, she projected how many pars and bogeys she needed to still break 80. She hoped she could continue to play well on the back nine, but knew her tendency was to stumble after a good score on the front nine. She thought, "Don't screw up the chance to break 80 with a double bogey."

Tina made a bogey on hole 10. She thought it was a hard hole and didn't expect to make a par, so it didn't bother her. After she parred holes 11 and 12, she felt confident and was more excited about breaking 80. On the tee box of hole 13, she thought ahead about par 5 on hole 15. She thought, "I can make birdie on 15 with a good drive in the fairway, which can really help me break 80." Because her mind was not focused on the now, Tina hit a bad tee shot and made a bogey on 13. By tee 14, she was two over par for the back nine and began to feel the pressure more than ever, because she knew that four over par on the back would break 80.

On the 14th tee, Tina said to herself, "Don't make a dumb mistake. Play it safe and hit it in the middle of the green." Tina was now protecting her score and afraid to make mistakes. She pulled a shot in the bunker and made another bogey. Instead of playing for birdie on the par-5 15th hole, she hit a 3-wood off the tee, laid up on her second shot, and hit it into the bunker on her third.

After hitting the ball in the bunker, Tina's blood was boiling. Bunker shots were not the strength of her game. She mentally sabotaged herself into another bogey with a poor sand shot and a missed par putt. She was four over par and needed pars on the last three holes to shoot 79. Since she was afraid to make a mistake on hole 16, she steered her tee shot into the woods and made double on the hole. She finished bogey, bogey on the last two holes to shoot 44 on the back and 83 for the day. But 83 was not the score Tina had hoped for after her performance on the front nine.

> *I screwed myself up when I said, "I'm 10 under and have three easy holes left, you can shoot 59," and sure enough I messed up. You can't think like that!*
>
> —SCOTT VERPLANK (CAREER LOW: 62)

Sally, on the other hand, takes a different approach, which is one reason she holds a 10-handicap. Sally shot 39 on the front nine. Unlike Tina, who was pleased with her good play on the front, Sally didn't like to pay attention to score. She thought focusing on scores limited her ability to play to her full potential. Her goal was to do her best on each shot. On hole 10, she focused on her drive only and did not pay attention to her past performance. Sally had learned how to take one shot at a time to not get ahead of herself and create a mental barrier.

Sally parred holes 10 and 11 but bogeyed holes 12, 13, and 14 with a bad tee shot on 12 and two loose approach shots on 13 and 14. But Sally did not let the bogeys upset her and interfere with her play on the next two holes. She knew she was playing well because she hit a lot of greens.

Despite playing what she thought was a good game, Sally resisted adding up her score. Her goal was to stick to her game plan and not play more aggressively or more conservatively because of her score. This strategy paid off on hole number 15 when she hit a second shot just short of the green, chipped close, and made a five-footer for birdie. She felt so confident on the next hole that instead of hitting an iron off the tee, she hit a driver over the corner of the dogleg. This was her only mental mistake of the day, and it cost her a double bogey on hole 16. After realizing her mental error, she decided to stick to her game plan on the last two holes. She finished with two pars and shot 39 on the back nine, 78 for the day.

As illustrated, Tina's attitude does not allow her to finish off a good round. She repeatedly commits the same mental errors that golfers typically make in this situation. She focuses too much on her score, thinks ahead about holes she has yet to play, places pressure on herself to shoot 79, and tries to protect her score on the back nine. Sally, on the other hand, doesn't let comfort zones affect her performance. She doesn't pay attention to score, tries to focus on one shot at time, sticks to her game plan, and stays composed when she makes an error.

> *When I get under par, I usually try to get more under. I don't just try to get it in the clubhouse.*
> —CHRIS TSCHETTER (CAREER LOW: 63)

A Close Call with 59

Most PGA and LPGA Tour pros don't usually fall victim to comfort zones. Professional athletes, however, are not immune to the same mental hazards amateurs experience. For example, tour pro Brian Claar had a chance to shoot 59 during the 1997 Hawaiian Open, but he became prey to his comfort zone and couldn't finish off the round when he encountered a long wait on the 11th tee.

Claar started his round by making six birdies in a row. For the first 10 holes, he was on cruise control and didn't realize he was eight under par. So far, to Claar, so good. However, what took him over two hours to play felt like only 20 minutes to Claar. Not unlike athletes who are playing in a comfort zone, Claar experienced a change in the perception of time. He should have recognized this shift in time as an indicator of playing in the zone.

On the 11th tee, while waiting to hit his tee shot, he had just enough time to think about his score. Before the wait, he was into a good rhythm: plan the shot, see it, hit it, and go find it and do it again. "Everything came to a logjam and everyone was talking about it and it got tough. I consciously started thinking about what I was shooting—before that I focused on what I needed to do," Claar said.

"At that point, shooting 59 entered my mind—I only need five more birdies. Then I started thinking ahead about the reachable par 5s and other holes I can birdie, and before you know it, I hit a 5-iron in the right bunker and made bogey. That got me back to reality pretty quick," Claar continued.

What happened to Claar's rhythm? During the first 10 holes Claar was focused on making birdies, playing shot by shot, and being totally immersed in the task of hitting shots. He realized he must be on the leader board, if not leading the tournament, when he heard others talking about how he was eight under par and noticed golf fans starting to gather around. Claar now became aware of his success and sensed the need to perform. He changed his focus, became defensive, and regressed into a protect mode. He became a victim of his comfort zone. The fear of blowing a good round was now more important than trying to make birdies.

Like Claar, the moment you begin to fear mistakes, you are in protect mode. Claar described the changes in his attitude: "I felt bulletproof for the first 10 holes. I felt like it was my day, but on hole 11 my attitude changed and I got defensive." Claar was familiar with the perils of playing safe. He knew how to avoid the pitfalls of the comfort zone. Despite his knowledge about playing in a protect mode, he began thinking about his score and sabotaged his chance of shooting a 59. The fact that he cared too much about score was the impetus that changed his focus and cost him the game. "In the back of your mind you still care too much," Claar said. A player who cares too much about score can't play in the now. Claar shot 62 that day, still a career round and a great start to the tournament.

He will always wonder what if—what if he had not waited on the 11th tee and lost the focus he had on the first 10 holes.

Don't Back Off; Never Back Off

Ernie Els was six under par through the 11th hole during the second round of the 1995 GTE Byron Nelson Classic. The realization of being in the middle of a great round could have affected his performance also, but he didn't let that fact hold him back. The goal was to keep the good round going and to avoid slipping into the comfort zone. Els described the round as being on "cruise control," which is a term players often use to describe playing in the comfort zone when performance feels effortless.

Like Els, every golfer arrives at a decisive moment in the game when play stops temporarily and you suddenly become aware of your performance and how well you are playing. Sometimes, just thinking about how well you are playing can jerk you out of cruise control. Even to seasoned pros, it is difficult not to analyze the round, calculate the score in relation to par, and think about the consequences of the round to the overall tournament. When you reach this point, how you respond to it determines your attitude for the rest of the round.

You think about score, it's hard not to. You don't want to make a mistake, make a bogey when you're playing well.

—STEVE JONES (CAREER LOW: 62)

When you realize how well you are performing, you can respond in two different ways. The first is to keep on pushing ahead, unaffected by the consequences of good or bad shots. The second is by protecting the score and playing safe. "Sometimes when you are six under par, you think, 'I am six under par—let's just hold on to this,'" Els concedes.

After Els finished the 12th hole during the second round of the 1995 GTE Byron Nelson Classic, he stood at seven under. This was a great score any day, but he had six holes remaining. At that moment in the round, he knew his attitude could be positive or destructive to his finish. "You can really push yourself in the positive way and go for a 61, or you might go the other way and hold on, where you say 'OK, I'm right in the tournament now—let's not blow it,'" Els said.

The most challenging obstacle is not based on physical performance. The toughest obstacle is the mental battle you fight when you are performing well. Stated Els, "I would say it's more mental than physical when you are playing well, because you have everything going for you. How did you get to seven under through 12? Because you hit good shots and you weren't thinking about score. From there on, you should just keep on going. It doesn't matter if you are trying to break 90 for the first time or shoot 59—the key is to let go of score, push yourself to go further, and not hold on. You build on the momentum. Don't back off; never back off. I think that's the key: you have to play fearless but still play percentage golf."

Get as Far Ahead as You Can

Ted Tryba is another example of a player who doesn't back down during a low round. Tryba, known for his work ethic and ability to go low often, shot his lowest score on the PGA Tour during the third round of the 1999 Los Angeles Open. After making birdie at hole number 10, he was five under par. No matter how many under par he was shooting, Tryba's attitude was that it wasn't low enough. His only purpose was to go to the next hole and try to get another chance at making birdie.

"I didn't once think that five under was low enough, or six under was low enough, or seven. It never even crossed my mind—I just felt like I had to keep going," Tryba said. Tryba's success is largely attributed to his mental attitude. His lack of concern about his score helps guard him from the restrictions of a comfort zone. Continued Tryba, "But I don't even realize I'm eight under. I knew, but I didn't care.

All I cared about was birdieing the next hole and what I had to do on the next hole." By avoiding the mental pitfalls of the comfort zone, Tryba was able to make eagle on 11 and birdie 12, 13, and 14 to go 10 under par for the day.

His goal, unlike other players in the same situation, was to get as far ahead as possible. "Still [after fourteen], I don't even think I'm 10 under for the round. I could care less, because now I'm right in this tournament. I've already got the lead—now I want to get as far ahead as I can," Tryba said. When he took the lead after 14 holes, this was Tryba's decisive moment in the round, but he didn't stop to contemplate his position. He was trying to run away and hide with the lead; there was no playing safe in him.

Tryba stayed with his game plan and didn't change his thinking. "I was just trying to get ahead, and just go, go, go. Birdies, one shot at a time, and play as well as you can. One of those things, where you know you got it going, and you got to let it go. You don't change your thought process at all. You just keep making birdie, execute, and birdie. That's all you think about," said Tryba. You might not be thinking about birdie, but instead about making another par.

You always have to realize when you have three or six holes to play, you can birdie all three or all six. Anything can happen.

—TED TRYBA

Tryba birdied hole 15 to get 11 under for the day. On hole 16, he started to think about shooting 59, his first mistake of the day. He turned his focus from the "now" and imagined that if he could get by hole 16 and birdie 17 or 18, he could shoot 59. He parred 16 and 17 and needed a birdie on 18 to shoot 59. Tryba hit a perfect tee shot in the middle of the 18th fairway. Never thinking about saving 60, he tried to hole his shot from the fairway. The shot looked perfect in the air, hit a hard spot short of the flag, and skipped to the back of the green in the rough. He finished the round with a 10-under-par 61. "I wish I could have played 36 holes that day, because I still would have been making birdies," Tryba said.

Turning a Good Round into a Great Round

Both Ted Tryba and Ernie Els know how to go low, as do many other pros, because they have been there before. They have broken all the mental barriers in golf, except breaking 60. They have learned how to play well when taking it deep, which has helped them shoot in the low 60s often. While you don't have their experience or ability, you can become a better player by learning from their mistakes and triumphs. The goal of this book is to help you play well all the time and to teach you to avoid retreating into your comfort zone when you have a potential career-low round under way.

Stop Caring About the Score

You learned in the earlier examples of an amateur golfer, Tina, and a golf pro, Brian Claar, that their downfall was in being score conscious. Score is the measure by which you judge your round. You use your score as a ruler to determine if it meets or exceeds your expectations. If you are oblivious to score, you won't compare it to what you expect to shoot.

Do everything in your power to avoid calculating your possible score for the day. You can't really care about score at that moment, but you can still try to play your best on each hole. How can you do this?

- Don't keep score during the round. Ask someone else in the group to keep score for you. At the end of the round, you can go back over each hole and add up the score.

- Don't play with a target score, or a particular score you want to shoot during the game. Instead, make it your goal to hit fairways and greens, and execute every shot to the best of your ability. The results will take care of themselves when you pay attention to the process. As Ted Tryba said, play one hole at a time and do the best you can on each shot.

Don't Safeguard Your Lead

The biggest error a golfer can make when going low is to become too protective of his or her score (or position). When you focus on your score (or position), you create a mental obstacle that forces you to play safe or defensive. You focus on how to avoid mistakes rather than on how to play well. You pay more attention to where the trees, out-of-bounds stakes, water, and bunkers are. Your fear of failure prohibits you from playing well, makes you control your swing, and causes you to lose momentum.

> *Once you get it going, it's definitely not the time to protect it. Go ahead and take advantage of the momentum. Go ahead and get as low as you can.*
>
> —JOHN HUSTON (CAREER LOW: 61)

The same phenomenon happens when a golfer takes the lead of the tournament or a basketball team gets a lead on the opposing team. The fear of blowing the lead makes the player change her strategy and mental focus. Ernie Els said, "Playing with a big lead—to me that's the toughest. You get a lead of five shots and others are now chasing you." Els thinks you have to do the same things that first got you in position to take the lead and not change your approach.

Every week on television, you can see players fold under the pressure of leading a tournament. Early in the week you see unknown players take the lead in the tournaments. But when Sunday comes, the pressure of leading a tournament and potentially winning causes them to reverse ground. These players have changed their focus from performing to the best of their ability to trying to stay in the lead position (or not screw up). Mentally, they have sabotaged their own play and success. To remain in a leading position, you can't change your focus and play safe to hold your position. The same idea holds true when you are playing a good round. You have to think the same, act the same, and play the same. Don't change your demeanor because the circumstances of the round are now more competitive.

Keep momentum on your side. Momentum can disappear quickly when you protect your score or play safe. When you have momentum in a round, take full advantage of it. However, you don't need to play as aggressively as John Daly does and go for broke on every shot in an attempt to maintain the momentum. Stay focused on trying to make solid pars (or bogeys). Keep the momentum going by playing within the bounds of your skills.

Rely on Your Game Plan

While it is important to maintain the momentum you built, great players such as Ernie Els recommend staying focused on playing smart golf even when emotions are high. No golfer, regardless of how good he or she is, should play with reckless abandon even when running on all cylinders. States Els, "It's an aggressive patience. You still must hit the percentage shot, but it's an aggressive shot. You have to stay aggressive and you have to push yourself to the absolute edge."

The tendency, when you have momentum on your side, is to abandon the game plan and play more aggressively, sometimes foolishly. This is what separates the great players from the followers. Els uses a game plan for every round and sticks to the game plan to avoid errors in play and losing momentum. The game plan for a 15-handicap should not change if you are 20 over par or five over par in the middle of a round. Play shots within the bounds of your limitations. If you can't hit the shot on the range successfully at least 50 percent of the time, then you had better hit a substitute shot. "Just keep yourself in the game and make good decisions. Play the right shots. I see so many people play the wrong shots all the time," Tryba says.

Try not to do too much. If you get a hard shot that you're not comfortable with, you just take the club that you feel like you can make your best swing with.

—JOHN HUSTON

What is a game plan? A game plan is a strategy you develop before the round that dictates your decisions on the golf course, such as what pin placements are easily accessible and what pins are inaccessible on approach shots. Els's game plan is to hit the ball in the fairway with whatever club gets the job done, play high-percentage shots into the greens by taking the trouble out of play, and relying on his putter. Don't be afraid to hit an iron off the tee to get the ball in play or lay up when you can't reach a par-4 green with water.

Your game plan should include clubs you can safely hit at any pin. In most situations, you should take dead aim at the flag with a short iron or wedge in your hand. Know when to pick a target in the middle of the green when you have a long iron in your hand and then rely on your putter. For example, if you have a long iron shot to a pin that is on the right edge of the green and you have to play over a bunker, aim 10 yards left of the flag toward the middle of the green. On the green, the plan is to be confident you can make any putt, no matter the distance.

Like many other pros, Steve Jones believes that you need a game plan, which should not change when playing good or bad. You shouldn't play more aggressively because you are trying to move up in position, trying to make up for a bogey, or just playing well. If Jones hits the ball well, his plan becomes more aggressive, but not foolish. Jones strives for what pros call "birdie opportunities." You might convert this into "par opportunities" (or "bogey opportunities") for your game. This means you should use a game plan that gives you the best chance to have a putt for par on every hole to avoid making bad decisions in the "heat of the battle."

A lot of times we're never aiming at the flags. We're looking for spots that are easier to putt—we don't want to get above the pin. We don't want to put ourselves in a bad spot.

—TED TRYBA (CAREER LOW: 61)

When John Huston gets a strong lead on the field, as happened at the Hawaiian Open, he practices smart golf. If you make a mistake or two, you don't want to panic and let your emotions cause more mistakes. Warns Huston, "Once you're in position to win the tournament, you just play smart. Try to keep the ball in play, and if you happen to make a bogey, it's no big deal, but you don't want to start to give back two or three shots at a time."

Doug Dunakey's 59: Making the Cut No Longer a Goal

Doug Dunakey was struggling on the Nike Tour before his brush with golf history in the middle of the 1998 season. Most golf fans remember him as "Almost Mr. 58," because he came within two feet of shooting the lowest score ever in a PGA-sanctioned event during the second round of the 1998 Nike Miami Valley Open. He became the second player in three weeks to shoot 59 on the Nike Tour. The previous players all did it on par-72 tracks. His 59 came on the par-70, 6,691-yard Heatherwoode Golf Club.

Starting the second round of the tournament at one under par, his goal was simply to make the cut, which he thought would take at least two under par. On the par-35 front nine, Dunakey needed only eight putts to shoot 27. He birdied six out of eight holes and made a 25-foot eagle chip on the par-5 fourth. After the fourth hole, he knew he was off the cut line, and it put him at ease. "The first nine holes was like a quiet calm. I made so many putts on the first nine holes it was kind of scary, because I started thinking about the 50s on the 10th tee," he said.

He continued his streak on the back nine by making birdie at holes 10 and 11. He parred the next two holes but came back with a birdie at 14. Now at 11 under par, all he had to do was par in for a 59, and he knew it. He recalls, "Usually when you shoot 59, you might birdie the last five or six holes and you come in strong. I had gotten to that level after 14 holes. I knew if I could par the last few, I could shoot 59, so those were probably the toughest five holes I've played."

Dunakey parred numbers 15 and 16 and was halfway there, but he went one better and birdied hole 17 to go to 12 under par. He now needed only a par on the finishing hole to shoot a 58. He hit his approach shot to about 25 feet from the cup, but then three-putted when he missed a two-footer for par. He finished second at the Miami Valley Open with respectable scores of 67 and 71 on the weekend. More important, he used it as a springboard to win the very next week at the Nike Cleveland Open, shooting 69-72 the first two rounds to make the cut on the number, then catching fire to go 65-65 on the weekend. "I felt like I had learned a little from last time," said Dunakey. Apparently, he had.

Fall Back on Something Positive

When Doug Dunakey thought about shooting 59 during the third round of the 1998 Nike Miami Valley Open, it was hard to stay focused on execution. He saw his name go from the bottom of the pack to the top of the leader board in 10 holes—a first for him all year. He was comfortable shooting low, but now he had the lead. "I could hear the people say 'Get the Golf Channel out here, because things are starting to happen.' That's when I felt, well, don't screw up," Dunakey said.

Dunakey focused on his preshot routine, which is a good idea for any player to do when it's hard to stay focused. "I tried to stay in my routine. That seems to keep me focused. It is something that you have relied on before. If I take nine seconds or whatever to do my routine, I try to keep that same rhythm, without doing a lot of thinking," Dunakey said. You already know from previous chapters that this helped him shoot 59 that day.

An excellent way to stay fixated on the process of execution (so you don't worry about score or results) is to stay in your routine. Your mind becomes occupied with the details of execution rather than overcome with worry about position or score. The mind can process only a finite amount of information at one time. When you fill your mind with something positive, it pushes out anxiety-producing thoughts. If you get nervous or start to worry about results, focus your mind on preshot preparation—picking a target, seeing and feeling a good shot, addressing the ball properly, and focusing on the target.

Final Thoughts

The mental attitude you need to finish off a good round is to stay the same. Don't change your mind-set because of the circumstances (playing well, playing better than expected, or leading the tournament). This means you should keep the same focus and play the same way you did on the front nine, relying on your game plan (your strategy for each hole) and locking your mind into something positive, such as the preshot routine.

1. Don't limit your performance with target scores. Try to focus on the process and doing your best, one shot at a time.

2. Don't change your attitude and play safe when you are playing well or are leading the tournament. Continue to play aggressively and take advantage of momentum, but don't step outside the limit of your skills.

3. Make a game plan for every round, which includes selecting targets off the tees, what strategy you will use to play each hole, and what process goals you want to accomplish for the round. Commit to the game plan no matter how well (or poorly) you are playing.

4. Lock your mind into something positive, like your preshot routine, when you feel pressure. Make sure you have a specific preshot routine for every shot. When your mind wanders to results, focus deeply on your routine to push out distractions.

Golfing with Perspective

When scoring well, for me I know I am going to trust it through right to the end.

—KATHRYN MARSHALL (CAREER LOW: 62)

Most people who are avid golfers regard golf as a critical component of their lives. If golf is a high priority for you, imagine how important it is to players who make a living playing it. Many pros play because they love the game, but their livelihood depends on how well they play every day. Making a game you love to play your career may sound like an ideal situation, but it has its pitfalls, too. When golf becomes a career for professionals, as it is for most tour pros, the purpose of the game changes and it becomes easier to lose perspective.

You and I have the luxury of playing golf for enjoyment. We don't have to worry about making cuts and playing on the weekends for our livelihood. We play because we love the game, like to be outside, enjoy playing with friends, and relish the rush of a well-struck shot. Some of us play to escape the doldrums of life; we want to get away from our regular routine and immerse ourselves in something that distracts us from the complications of life. Some people play to gain accolades from others to satisfy the need to feel liked and respected; others use the sport as a way to network for business purposes. Some people play merely for the thrill of the competition and the emotions that come from a good battle.

The reason you play golf shapes your attitude and perspective on the golf course. If you love competition and your main goal is to win at golf, it's more than just a social game for you. You play to compete and score the best you can. When your motivation to play golf is based upon your desire to win, you are more vulnerable to becoming consumed by the pressure to play well and win. When you become consumed by pressure, be it the pressure of social interaction, the pressure of your expectations, or the pressure of winning and playing well, it's easier to lose perspective. If you are without a healthy perspective on golf, your game will ultimately suffer.

Every autumn, professional golfers compete to qualify for their respective tours. One of the most intense weeks in a tour professional's life occurs during the PGA Tour, the LPGA Tour, and the Senior PGA Tour Qualifying Schools, or Q-Schools, which determine who qualifies to play on the Tours. Q-School is all about survival. The stakes are high, because one week may change a player's life and career forever. One bad swing or missed three-footer can mean the difference between playing for $5,000 each week on minitours or $2.5 million a week on the PGA Tour.

I've helped players qualify for the Tours. I've also helped players deal with the frustration of "flunking" Q-School. The pressure to make it on tour is great, because if a player does well, his or her life can change forever. Qualifying School is the toughest and most pressure-packed week for players who feel that golf is the only thing they can do or want to do in their lives. Most players devote the entire year to preparing their games to play well during tour qualifying. For thousands of PGA Tour, LPGA Tour, and Senior Tour hopefuls who want to get to the finals and earn a playing card, it's very hard to hold up under the pressure. Every golfer knows what's at stake, and the thought of failing makes the week even more frightening. It's difficult to play well when you feel that your career may be on the line for at least the next year.

Just like your pro counterparts, you also play with pressure. However, your pressure is slightly different from that of your pro counterparts. Your pressure comes from making golf too important in your life. In this chapter, you'll learn how to keep golf in perspective and approach life with more balance so you can play with less pressure, less anxiety, and more fun. You'll discover how tour pros shot career-low rounds by golfing with perspective, and you will learn how your golfing mind-set and your ability to shoot a low round is influenced by your reasons for playing golf.

Golfing from a healthy perspective means that you define what values are most important to you, where golf fits into your list of priorities, and what needs to happen to maintain a balance in your life. A person who has a balanced life is in a better position to golf with perspective. When I work with young, aspiring tour golfers, I always discuss the concept of balance in their lives. I realize that a balanced life will make my students happier and at the same time circumvent some of the pressure they feel about succeeding in golf. Most of the aspiring tour golfers I work with make their golf career such a high priority that they often lose sight of other aspects in their lives that are equally important. This precludes students from maintaining a healthy perspective when they play; they have put too much pressure on themselves to succeed at golf.

Golf fanatics who eat, sleep, and play golf every day are more prone to adopt an unhealthy perspective. So much time is devoted to playing good golf that they lose sight of the joy of playing the sport they love. Where most amateur golfers differ is that they treat golf as a game to enjoy, to have fun playing with friends, and they take pleasure from competition. As an amateur golfer, missing a three-foot putt should not be a life-or-death event for you, nor should your golf career depend on the number of putts you make or miss.

If you make golf too important in the overall scheme of your life, you golf with an unhealthy perspective. When you care too much about your golf performance, three-putting the first green of the day may be a major source of frustration. If missing a putt becomes too important, golf can consume you, which leads to more stress and an unbalanced life. Golfing with an unhealthy perspective also means that you might be too serious, try too hard to play well, expect more and more from yourself all the time, or worry about how others judge you based on your golf performance. When your golf performance becomes most important, other areas of your life suffer, leading to a less fulfilled and less satisfying life.

A balanced perspective is crucial to shooting low scores. If too much importance is placed on winning or playing well, your performance will ultimately suffer. You will not be able to play up to your potential because you are blocked by fear, doubt, expectations, and self-induced pressure. When you release yourself from the mental shackles of seriousness, your performance will improve and you will have more fun with a game that you used to play just for fun.

Eight Signs That Golf Is Too Important

As with any obsession, there are warning signs that can help you identify whether or not your golf perspective is unhealthy. The most common symptoms of an unhealthy golf perspective are the following:

1. Other facets of your life suffer because you are so immersed in golf. You are similar to the workaholic who spends all of his or her waking hours at work with no "free time." When you become a golfaholic, work, family, and other relationships ride in the backseat of your golf cart.

2. Your daily routine is arranged around golf practice and play. The first and foremost goal each day is to practice or play golf. Your schedule revolves around when you need or want to practice or play.

3. Golf consumes your conscious mind. When you are not playing, practicing, or shopping for new equipment, your mind is active with thoughts about playing or practicing golf. You have golf on the brain all the time.

4. You feel upset (guilty, depressed, angry) unless you are doing something to improve your game or something that involves golf. You are happy only when you are playing, practicing, or doing something to improve your game. The guilt of doing something

other than working on your game is too strong to let you enjoy other activities.

5. You're obsessed with playing well all the time. Like a perfectionist, you do not accept mediocrity or bad golf. Making a mistake such as missing a short putt makes you very frustrated with yourself. You set higher and more difficult goals for yourself after you reach new goals.

6. You are addicted to the competition that comes with playing golf. You feel like the drug addict who needs a fix. The thrill of competition acts like a drug on you, and you will do anything to get your high. Nothing else excites you like a good golf match.

7. You constantly feel like giving up golf altogether, because it gives you heartache when you don't play as well as expected. You often feel stuck, depressed, or alone because your performance does not match your expectations. You want to give up the game because you can't play up to your unrealistic expectations.

8. You practice and play so much golf that you are a candidate for burnout. You often feel tired and anxious because of the mental and physical demands of golf and your lack of time off from golf and/or time to renew. Trying harder and practicing more sometimes does not pay off. Instead you burn out.

Don't worry if you fit the profile of any of the above signs. There are solutions to gaining back a healthy perspective, which will be discussed later in this chapter.

Life-Altering Events Change Perspective

When a major change occurs in someone's life, such as a death, divorce, birth, or life-threatening disease, a person's perspective changes instantly. In the fall of 1999, the golf world was rocked by the senseless death of Payne Stewart when his private plane crashed. For those who knew Stewart or were close to him, the news was certainly shocking and difficult to comprehend. When a person close to you dies, it shakes up your life. You are suddenly forced to step back and closely examine your own existence, as many golfers did after Stewart's tragic death. As you contemplate your own mortality, it brings into focus what is important in your life.

I spoke with many golfers after Stewart's fatal accident who said that his death gave them a different perspective on life and the importance of golf in their lives. When tragedy strikes, people realize just how temporary their lives are and desire to make changes to improve them. Suddenly, golf is not important in the overall game of life.

PGA Tour star David Duval has always kept golf in perspective. In an interview after Stewart's death, he said, "[During] the five years I have played [tour golf], golf is not terribly important to me. It is not the biggest thing in my life. And again, it still isn't. It never has been." Keeping a healthy perspective is probably why Duval is one of the dominant players on the PGA Tour today. Maybe Duval learned this lesson the hard way when tragedy struck in his own life: he lost his younger brother to a rare disease.

Even your own misfortune can help you make positive changes in your life. When disaster affects you personally, such as when you contract an illness like cancer, a shift in your thinking occurs. This is especially true if you have lived a healthy life and then suddenly become ill. You are forced to evaluate your life, goals, and current situation, which usually lead to a new perspective on life and a better way of living. It's a tough lesson to learn, but many people make positive life changes only after a personal tragedy, improving their health by eating a better diet or starting a long-term exercise program, for example.

How would your life change if you were diagnosed with a terminal illness and had only one year to live? It's a difficult question to answer but one that is at the heart of this discussion. Would you change the way you live, and if so, how? How important would golf be to you? Most people in this situation would do everything in their power to fight the illness. Priorities would change. Health would become the number-one priority. You would do what's most important to you, depending on your personal values.

A more positive example of how your priorities can change quickly is when you experience the birth of a child. Some tour players I've worked with over the years have married and had children. I often hear them say, "Missing a three-foot putt is not as terrible as it used to be before the birth of our first child." If you have children or know others who do, you see how one's outlook can change quickly after the birth of a child, especially a first child. That's why it's called an "eye-opener." I know this from experience, because recently my wife and I had our first child.

Tragedy Puts Golf in Perspective

Kathryn Marshall is an example of a golfer who was enlightened by tragedy. In 1997, she shot 62 in the second round of the State Farm Rail Classic, the lowest score of her career, and tied for the LPGA record for an 18-hole score. Marshall's first-round 72 had placed her in the middle of the tournament field at the end of the day. She told me the second round was the most memorable round of her life, not because of the score she shot but because of what she learned had happened the night before the second round. After the first round, she heard that Princess Diana had died in a car accident, an event that shocked the entire world. Marshall considered Diana to be a good friend. "It was a very memorable round," Marshall said. "It was a sad day because I found out that Princess Diana died. I was amazed by how affected I was by the news. It was a sad occasion, and it put everything into perspective."

After Marshall heard the sad news, golf seemed less important. Princess Diana's catastrophe made her very sad, but ironically it helped her to relax and forget about the pressure of making the cut. "It was funny, because there I was worrying about making the cut when someone had just been killed in a car crash. It really took any pressure I had off my game, and I felt if it's going to happen, it's going to happen," she said.

Usually Marshall is a very intense, passionate player on the course, but that day her demeanor was more relaxed and less serious. Trying to make the cut, worrying about scoring well, and being too intense on the golf course—all very negative attitudes—were erased overnight when she was forced to look at the role of golf in her life. Because she was moved by tragedy, Marshall was on her way to forming a healthy perspective about golf. "I wasn't worried about my score because I was taken with Diana's death, and it was ho-hum golf—a very laid-back attitude. I wish I could incorporate that into my game every day, because we are all trying like crazy to do well out here. Usually I'm too hyper, intense," Marshall said.

Marshall brought up an important issue: caring too much. Golfers who care too much about their score or performance sometimes are not able to play up to their potential. I often point out for my clients the distinction between "caring" and "trying." *Caring* means you want to play well, are focused too much on score and your performance. With this attitude, you are too tense and serious about your game. This places unnecessary pressure on you and translates into worry, trying too hard, and having unrealistic expectations.

Trying, on the other hand, simply means you want to play well but it is not a burning desire that alters your life. You still concentrate on golf and give it your best. "A lot of people can learn that there is no need to worry," Marshall said. "Obviously, we take golf very seriously and playing relaxed is easier said than done, but you have to really relax and trust in yourself."

The key for Marshall was to stop caring about golf. When she stopped caring too much, it was easier to play golf free of expectations and worry. However, in the second round of the State Farm Rail Classic, she had a great round going and was throwing a no-hitter. The round transformed from an attempt to make the cut to suddenly playing in contention for the tournament. As discussed earlier, as soon as a player realizes what's at stake (a possible career-low round or winning), caring goes to work again and the round becomes too important. She said, "I thought I was going to birdie in for a 59. And then I hit a shot 20 yards off-line, chipped up, and missed the putt completely." This was an indication that she was starting to lose her relaxed perspective.

She was able to regain her focus on the last few holes and finish with a career-low 62. Many players in the same situation (six under after 11 holes) would let the pressure to perform well take over and make a big number, but her confidence wasn't going to allow that to happen. "When scoring well, for me I know I am going to trust it through right to the end," Marshall said. "You hear a lot about players who are playing really well and then all of a sudden they have an eight or nine on the card and blow up. For me that would be the last thing I was doing because I was completely in control that day."

Great Amateur Rounds

Twelve-year-old Henry Liaw of Rowland Heights, California, stood only 5'6", but he could hit 250-yard drives routinely. Henry picked up the game at age nine and just a year later won his first junior tournament. In 1998, he shot an incredible 12-under 58. Liaw, who plays with tons of confidence, won almost every junior tournament in Southern California in his age group in 1998. His amazing 58 at Alhambra Municipal Golf Club has been the pinnacle of his young golfing career. The par-70 layout in Southern California is only 5,214 yards from the back tees, but Liaw still had to hit the shots and make putts to shoot 58. He became the first junior golfer to shoot a competitive round in the 50s on an SCPGA regulation course.

Henry favors golf over every sport. "In team sports, if something bad happens, it could be somebody else's fault. In golf, you do well, and you win. You don't, and you blame yourself," Liaw said. His 58 included 10 birdies, an eagle, and only 25 putts. With his uncanny ability to hit straight shots, Liaw only missed one green. More recently, he shot a 66 at Industry Hills near Los Angeles, where he holds the course record of 65.

J. D. McNeill is another young phenom to watch for. A high school junior, McNeill shot a course-record nine-under-par 62 to win the Optimist tournament. Later he was told he had beaten the previous course record, set by Sam Snead in a pro-am more than 40 years ago. "I couldn't believe he was the one who held the record," said McNeill. His previous best round had been a 68. McNeill's record round consisted of two bogeys, nine birdies, and an eagle. He played the last 14 holes at nine under par. On the last hole of the day, J.D. made a six-foot eagle putt to better Snead's 40-year-old mark. His longest putt of the day was just 10 feet. Watch out, Tiger Woods and David Duval.

Connecting with Your Values

By now you understand that having a more carefree attitude helps you play better. By not caring so much about results, score, and how you perform, you can take the pressure off. The big question is this: how do you care less about outcomes without undermining your motivation? In addition, how can you take a more balanced approach to life and be less "golf-centered"? The place to start is identifying your values in life and deciding what's important to you.

> *In the back of your mind you still care too much. If you can feel you have nothing to lose, it's not a big deal if you hit a bad shot. I think that would be the best way to play.*
>
> —BRIAN CLAAR

What are values? Values are beliefs you hold closest to your heart. They are the principles and ideals by which you live your life. Values influence the choices you make, color your perceptions, influence the goals you have, and direct you toward a life you desire. Identifying your values can help you (1) make better decisions, (2) improve your well-being, (3) manage your time and energy better, (4) know yourself better, and (5) act in line with your ideal values. Often beliefs, behaviors, or values become habits of thinking because people don't stop to consider the reasons for the things they do or say.

Before you think about your values, it may be helpful to "begin with the end in mind"[1] by thinking about your purpose in life. What is most important in your life? How do you see or imagine yourself at the end of your life? What would you want others to say about you at your funeral? I don't mean to be morbid, but these questions force you to examine your life values: where you are now and what you want to achieve before you get to the end of your life feeling unfulfilled.

What values are most important for you? Values can motivate you, drive you, excite you, or make you feel fulfilled or happy. Here are a few examples of values that you might live by:

- To seek adventure
- To feel happy
- To live a healthy life
- To contribute to society
- To be a competent parent
- To be a loving husband or wife
- To create or build things
- To seek pleasure
- To feel connected to others
- To teach others
- To be a leader to others
- To discover and learn
- To gain wealth
- To lead a spiritual life

I already know that mastering golf is a high priority for you, or you wouldn't have picked up this book. What values are important to you outside of your golf game? Pick five or more values that you want to live by and influence how you behave on a daily basis. Remember that the purpose of this exercise is to look beyond the game of golf and create a balanced approach to your life.

---

1. Taken from *The Seven Habits of Highly Effective People* (1989).

The next step is to identify the goals you have for your life based on your life purpose statement. This statement defines your values and identifies your life purpose: what you want to accomplish in life. List five or more goals you want to accomplish in your life, such as "be a good parent to my children." Are your goals in line with your values? If so, that's great! If your goals are not in line with your values, you need to set new goals that support your values.

The final step is to honor your values by living a life you want free of what others perceive is right or wrong for you. One of the roadblocks to personal success and happiness is trying to satisfy other people's expectations. Do you play golf because you want to play the game, or do you play because it brings happiness to others around you? Your aspirations should be your own and not the aspirations of others.

Playing Golf with a Balanced Life

Whether you are a high-handicap weekend golfer or a scratch amateur golfer, golfing with perspective will help you play better, enjoy yourself more, and maintain a more positive attitude about golf. When you make golf too important or serious, you lose perspective about where golf fits in your life.

I'm not saying you should change your desire to practice and improve, to give up your goals of winning at golf or dreaming about playing the best you can. If you take my message to the extreme, it can cripple your motivation to succeed. The intention is to help you play better by discovering the realization that golf does not have to be the focus or center of your life (although it may feel that way when you're immersed in a good round). I want you to search for a balance in life, have other outlets for satisfying your competitive urges, and be able to play in a relaxed state of mind and free of self-imposed pressures to succeed.

Golf Is Not a Reflection of Who You Are

I often ask my students to make an important distinction in their life. I want them to be able to detach performance (score, golf ability) from how they view themselves or from their self-esteem. For various reasons, golfers are notorious for attaching how they feel about themselves as a person to how well they perform each day in golf. If you do this, it means that you feel good about yourself (have self-esteem) only when you play well. Likewise, it means you feel bad about yourself after playing poorly. You accept the false belief that how successful you are in any endeavor (golf, work, family, or other areas) is directly linked to your self-worth. It's easy to fall prey to this belief, because that's the message our culture bombards us with every day.

Society teaches us that success is the foundation for self-worth, which I think is wrong. Can you feel good about yourself only if you are successful in some endeavor? I hope not. Take away that success and how do you feel as a person? Self-esteem should be based on your values as a person and what personal characteristics identify you. The people in your life will still love you because they enjoy you as a person, not just because you are a good golfer or successful businessperson.

Broadening Your Roles

Sometimes you get lost in the bigger picture of life because you become too absorbed in one role in your life. Some golfers I work with define themselves as golfers without giving credit or importance to the other roles in their lives, such as husband or wife, father or mother, or friend. It's easy to become absorbed in the role of a golfer and forget other, equally important, roles. For tour professionals, everything outside of golf revolves around golf—job, family, friends, and other businesses. Friends and associates reinforce this because they relate to this person only through the topic of golf. Remember that your life is not defined by you as the golfer only.

Creating Balance in Your Life

You never want to risk everything on one endeavor. The same is true when you are developing a healthy perspective about golf in your life. Balance in your life comes from four basic areas: (1) self-care—your health and well-being, (2) relationships—family and friends, (3) career—striving for career goals, and (4) recreation—hobbies, vacations, and other activities you enjoy. This list may not include every situation in your life, but it covers the most important ones. Without good health, it's difficult to thrive in all other areas in your life. Thus, your health and well-being must be a priority. For example, if you are injured or sick, you may be prevented from playing golf altogether.

People are social beings, too. We have a need to be loved by others, to have relationships and friends, to socialize with others. Every person wants to be able to share their success and happiness with people who are important to them.

People are also motivated to strive for success—to be the best they can be in an endeavor. This is a priority for a lot of people who are success-driven. Many people are driven by the need to be successful in the workplace. Be it a promotion, a raise, a special award or recognition, we all want to achieve certain goals in our career path.

Last, people need time to renew their minds and bodies. You can call it an escape, time off, rest period, vacation, or whatever. People need to get away from the mundane routines of daily life so they can come back with a clear mind, a rested body, and a fresh attitude.

Working the Process Brings Results

I always tell my students that pressure comes from worry about results. When you worry about outcomes (score for a hole, score for 18 holes, winning, or losing) and have an extreme need to gain those outcomes, your performance suffers. You don't realize how you burden yourself with subtle self-sabotage. If playing well, for whatever reason, is an extreme need, your attention is on achieving good results, and thus you may become too focused on the outcome instead of the process that will lead to your goal.

When Al Geiberger shot 59, he was more focused on breaking the Tour record for eight consecutive birdies than shooting 59. Without a hole-by-hole focus, he said the pressure to shoot 59 would have been too great to handle: "As I look back on it, trying to break the Tour record of eight under for eight holes was the best thing that could have happened to me. . . . Going for that goal within the round took my mind off my eventual score and got me past the choking point."[2] Remember that working the process is the best method for achieving good outcomes. For example, thinking about making (or missing) a putt for par is an outcome focus. Thinking about the ingredients of the tasks that will lead to making the putt is a process focus. Peak performance flows from a process focus—being immersed in the smaller tasks that lead to good outcomes.

Expectations and Golfing with Perspective

If you watch professionals play, you have noticed they make golf look easy. You see David Duval shoot 59 and Tiger Woods shoot 62. This tends to raise the standard and increase the average golfer's perceptions about what is possible. "If the pros can shoot in the low 60s, I should be able to break 90," you say to yourself. Playing par golf is standard for the professionals, but not for most weekend golfers. You can't compare your performance to that of professionals. As I've discussed, it's best not to use target scores or keep any expectations about what should be a good score for you. Expectations are another subtle form of self-sabotage, because they force you to judge how you are playing by how you think you should be playing. Again, this leads to thinking about your possible score while you are playing and is another form of outcome thinking, which, as we discussed, is not conducive to playing process golf.

Final Thoughts

I've talked at length about how to gain a better perspective through balance in one's life and not placing so much importance on your golf performance. This idea is directed at the very motivated and driven golfers—those I call overmotivated players. But many golfers *underperform* because they are on the opposite side of the motiva-

---

2. From Al Geiberger's *Tempo: How to Find It and How to Keep It* (1980).

tion continuum—they are undermotivated players. I have not addressed undermotivated golfers because they don't have the same problems as overmotivated golfers, but undermotivation has its own problems. When I talk about an undermotivated player, I am referring to a player who does not set high goals for his or her game, does not like to practice, and takes a more carefree approach to playing. Although the undermotivated golfer is able to relax and have more fun playing, he or she lacks the motivation and commitment to become a better golfer.

The point is that once you are on the golf course, you should be immersed in playing the game. Commit yourself fully to playing instead of feeling that you should be spending time with your children or doing something else. Some people use golf as a distraction or escape from the doldrums of life, and that's OK. But once you hit your first tee shot, make the best of the round (and day) without feeling guilty about playing, worrying about work, or anticipating what needs to get done. Once you lace up your golf shoes and grab the golf bag, temporarily transform into the role of the "golfer." You are still a family person, businessperson, and brother or sister, but for four hours you will commit to enjoying your time playing golf.

EIGHT

Going Low Again and Again

I could shoot 59 every day I go out to play.
—NOTAH BEGAY (CAREER LOW: 59)

John is a talented high school golfer who consistently and comfortably shoots in the mid-70s. He's shot even par or one under par so many times on the front nine only to shoot over par for 18 holes that he doesn't understand why he can't break par as consistently as he can shoot between 74 and 78. John has succeeded in breaking par for 18 holes only once in his life. He attributed this to playing in optimal weather conditions and an easy course. He wants to break par more often, but he's mentally blocked from shooting below par because he doesn't view himself a par golfer, can't play outside of his comfort zone, and has a fear of success, as well as the expectations associated with an ability to perform well.

John does not view himself as a par golfer. Instead, he is comfortable viewing himself as a "mid-70s golfer." Although he often has stretches of brilliant performance on the golf course, he finds a way to play to his handicap. If he has a chance to break par, he will make a couple bogeys on the last few holes and shoot a score that is reflective of his handicap. The one time he did break par, he didn't take it seriously. He couldn't accept his score for what it was and rejected the legitimacy of his personal-best score.

Because he doesn't think outside of his comfort zone, John never expects to shoot anything better than in the mid-70s, and this becomes a self-fulfilling prophecy. A good score on the front nine is usually erased with negative thoughts of hitting bad shots on the back nine. John sabotages his performance when playing well by thinking thoughts such as "When am I going to make double and mess up another good round?" He reinforces the assumption that he cannot play any better when he makes a double. Suddenly, his hunch becomes reality and he doesn't finish the round off strongly.

John also plays with the misconception that if he shoots more scores under par, the coach will move him to number one on his high school team. However, he doesn't want the pressure to play in the number-one spot on the team. The fear of not living up to the expectations from his coach and teammates is too much to handle, and he doesn't want to feel he has to carry the team's performance. He would rather play in the number-two or -three spot, where he won't feel the pressure to produce for the team. (Later in this chapter, I'll discuss John's mental roadblocks to success and provide some suggestions to getting beyond those roadblocks.)

Successful athletes, performers, and business professionals all have one common quality: they see themselves as possessing the skills necessary to excel in their chosen career. This is known as "positive self-image." Both self-image and self-confidence are core personality characteristics that greatly influence one's behavior. Self-image is based on how you honestly describe your own character. Self-confidence is how you perceive your ability to perform a given task. Successful people have an image of themselves as triumphant and have an enormous amount of self-confidence in their ability to be successful. For example, if you asked the best shooters in the NBA who's the best shooter or the best hitters in major league baseball who's the best hitter, each player would identify himself as the best. This perception applies to athletes in all sports, including golfers.

Your self-image as a golfer influences your ability to shoot low and to continue to shoot low scores. While doing research for *The Mental Art of Putting*, I asked many players from each of the pro tours who the best putters are. Senior PGA Tour player Bob was one player I interviewed. I asked Murphy, "Who is the best putter on the Senior Tour?" What do you think he said? He pointed to himself and said, "I am the best putter on this tour." You might say that he sounds arrogant. However, that's a sign of true confidence—something you must possess to succeed in any sport. It also says a lot about his self-image as a player and as a great putter. This is a common trait found in all great golfers.

You also have a self-image as a golfer. Embedded in that self-image is your perception of a personal "scoring zone." A scoring zone identifies what you are capable of shooting on any given day. For example, if you usually score between 92 and 98, you have an image of yourself as a "90s shooter." This expectation of a particular score range (e.g., 92–98) is the starting point of your comfort zone, as it defines what score you perceive you are most capable of playing on any given day. As discussed in Chapter 1, an expectation, whether based on performance or score, becomes self-defeating when you play better than expected or after you break 90 for the first time.

Breaking Away from Personal Scoring Zones

A scoring zone does not mentally restrict most tour players, because they know that preconceptions will limit their performance. A tour player has an image of himself or herself as a good player who can shoot par or better every day, but he or she isn't constrained by the notion of a scoring zone. All tour players have to break through important scoring milestones. You have to do the same in order to progress as a golfer and continue to shoot lower and lower scores. Breaking 100 is a big hurdle for a beginner or a very young golfer. The next scoring milestones are breaking 90, 80, par, 70, 65, and 60, with only a handful of golfers who have broken 60.

A new self-image is formed once a pro breaks into the 60s and shoots a few rounds in the mid-60s. All previous scoring milestones were broken (except for breaking 60, which is very rare in golf). The player accepts shooting low, then forms a new self-image and reaches a new level of confidence. Scoring low was not an accident, because it was done repeatedly. There are no obstacles to what a pro can shoot except for his or her preconceived beliefs of what he or she is capable of shooting.

> *There are no limits to what you can do, except for your own*
> *self-imposed limits.*
>
> —SCOTT VERPLANK

Tour pro Notah Begay is an example of a player who broke away from the limitations of a personal scoring zone. As mentioned earlier, Begay was the first Nike Tour player to record a 59 in tournament play, at the 1998 Nike Dominion Open. Begay is no stranger to shooting low scores. In college, he shot scores of eight, nine, and 10 under par, the last a record 62 during the 1994 NCAA Tournament in McKinney, Texas, to help Stanford win the NCAA title. He knew one day he had the potential to shoot a 59 in competition and that it was only a matter of time. Begay said, "I've never been short of confidence. I think I can shoot 58 someday. Records are made to be broken, aren't they?"

Begay's 59 really surprised a lot of people, because at the time he was just a conditional player on the Nike Tour struggling to make cuts. As a conditional player, he could enter and play only one out of the first seven events, which wasn't enough time to get into a rhythm of playing tournament golf. At the Nike Dominion Open, he shot two under the first round of the tournament. His goal starting the second round was to make the cut and get to play on the weekend. He certainly wasn't trying to shoot 59, nor was it a target score. Seven holes into the second round, he was just two under par for the day and four under for the tournament. He knew a strong back nine would ensure that he made the cut. "I made a 30-footer on eight and two-putted for birdie on nine. So I get to six under for the tournament, then I switched from making the cut to getting into contention. I eagled 10, birdied 11, and aced 12. So I went from four to nine under in just three holes."

Although he was very familiar with shooting low scores in college, Begay wasn't used to the pressure of being in contention to win a professional golf tournament. Even so, he handled it very well. "Walking off 12 green I wasn't thinking, 'Oh God, just get [my score] to the clubhouse.' I was thinking about going low. I didn't care where the ball went. I just tried to hit it as hard as I could and make another birdie." Begay knew it was the wrong time to start thinking about winning the tournament; he was in the groove and continued to play in it.

As you win golf tournaments, you're exposed to more situations. So, therefore, the next time you have a chance, you will probably encounter something very similar and you know how you dealt with it, the feelings you had, how you worked through it.

—DAVID DUVAL

A smart player realizes she has to go with the flow when in the midst of a low round and ride it all the way to the clubhouse. "When you get [in the groove], you get out of your own way and allow yourself to become a free spirit," Begay said. He knows, like other pros, that when shooting seven or eight under par you must keep going and not play conservatively. As Begay settled in over the shot, the greens seemed to enlarge; he focused on rhythm and balance and just cocked and swung. "When you know you're in that zone [in the groove], kick it while it's down. Every golfer who has ever played the game knows that it will kick you when you're down," Begay said.

Notah Begay has the confidence to believe it's possible to shoot a low number every day he plays, but he doesn't expect it to happen every day. He understands that too many outside factors or intangible elements affect one's day-to-day performance. His confidence is certainly a reflection of his past ability to go low, but it's also a reflection of his self-image as a golfer: that he has the ability and skills to shoot low scores any day he plays. "I think it's possible to shoot a low number anywhere. I'm still looking for that 57. It's out there, I know it's out there," said Begay.

Unlike top tour pros, amateurs stop themselves short of breaking new scoring milestones because they bring into play self-defeating labels and lack of confidence. For example, if you label yourself as a 90-plus player, that label becomes a self-fulfilling prophecy, which prevents you from breaking 90 when you are in the midst of a good round. Like the example of John, the belief is "No matter what I do, I find a way to shoot in the 90s." Therefore, when you do break 90 for the first time, that core belief prevents you from moving to the next level—you beat yourself—and your scoring self-image remains a "90s player." You might credit the good round to luck or to the ease of the course. This only serves to justify the core belief: "I'm not good enough to shoot in the 80s." What are some of the specific beliefs that prevent golfers from moving to the next level and believing they are good enough to shoot lower scores? Let's examine a few of them.

Mind-Sets That Keep You Stuck in a Scoring Range

Do you have trouble taking compliments to heart? Do you downplay even small accomplishments? Are you an extreme pessimist? The first behavior that prevents you from developing confidence and a positive self-image is when you "disqualify the positive." The tendency to disqualify the positive, such as when you downplay achievements, is often a side effect of perfectionism. Perfectionists are very hard on themselves. Even small successes are not recognized as a positive step, because perfectionists demand so much from themselves.

It is sometimes very difficult to strengthen your confidence if you can't take pride in and reward yourself for small achievements or for reaching even modest goals. If you disqualify the positive, the first time you break a scoring milestone such as 100 or 90, you can't take pride in your achievement and gain confidence. You may be happy with your newfound triumph for a short time, but then you quickly get back on the bandwagon of criticism and self-judgment.

The second behavior that prevents people from continuing to shoot lower scores is attributing success (and failure) to luck. Attribution theory is what psychologists define as an individual's perceptions of the causes of events and outcomes and provides clues about a person's personality and future behavior. Generally, people strive for success and try to avoid failure. We attribute outcomes or the reasons for success and failure to one of four causes: effort, ability, difficulty of the task, and luck. Ability and effort are believed to be under a person's control, whereas task difficulty and luck are typically not. Because ability level does not change from day to day, effort is seen as the most controllable attribute for outcomes.

If you think that a low round in golf is attributable to playing an easy course or just good luck (both beyond your control), it's harder to develop confidence and a positive self-concept. You don't take responsibility for your success (or failure) in a task, which leads to a state of learned helplessness. Learned helplessness makes you feel like giving up in the face of failure because you perceive that the cause of failure is out of your control. You attribute failure to lack of ability ("I don't have the ability"), luck ("It was an unlucky round"), or difficulty of the task ("I played on a difficult course"). Thus, you also perceive that breaking 100 or 90 for the first time was a result of good fortune or because you played an easy course, not ability level or amount of effort. Attributing your low round to luck or other factors beyond your control makes it difficult for you to gain confidence and be optimistic about your success, which prevents you from breaking new barriers.

The third behavior that prevents golfers from continuing to shoot low scores is fear of success. You would think that most people want to be successful at whatever they attempt to do, including playing golf. Curiously, many people sabotage their own success just when success may be close. This is called *self-sabotaging behavior*. People sabotage their chances for success to avoid dealing with the underlying fears that come with success. Because it can be an unconscious process, many people who have fear of success are not even aware of it.

I like being secure, but it is strange when you have all this money but you can't go into a mall and spend it.

—LARRY BIRD

At high-profile levels of the game of golf, you can understand that success has its drawbacks. Tiger Woods became a huge success early in his career, but with success came other problems. His superstardom could easily have derailed his career if he was not prepared to cope with it ahead of time. He dealt with stardom very well but has had to deal with the many other problems that come with fame, especially at his level of celebrity. For example, Woods has had to (and continues to) deal with being under the scrutiny of the public eye, demands from media and golf fans, as well as the golfing community's high expectations of his play. Just appearing out in public becomes a daily challenge for Woods, because he is recognized wherever he goes.

Some people might like the types of problems Woods experiences because of his celebrity status. For others, the fear of success and the complications that come with success are as strong as the fears associated with the fear of failure. Many successful athletes, performers, and businesspeople have sabotaged their careers because of the fear of success.

One example of a person who engaged in self-sabotaging behavior resulting from the fear of success is hockey star Derek Sanderson,[1] who started his career with the Boston Bruins. Derek won Rookie of the Year honors with Boston and helped his team win two Stanley Cup Championships in his first five years with the team. Now on top of the hockey world, he signed a contract with Philadelphia worth $2.65 million, which was far better than what he was paid in Boston ($50,000 per year). After signing the contract, he felt he didn't deserve the huge sum of money he was paid and tried to abolish his guilt with alcohol and drugs. His performance suffered, and he ended up losing $15 million because of legal fees and some bad business moves.

---

1. From The Success Syndrome: Hitting Bottom When You Reach the Top (1986).

Why might the fear of success affect your performance if you play golf only for recreation and not as a career? While you probably don't have to deal with the fear of public scrutiny if you win a club championship, you might sabotage yourself by harboring more subtle fears of success, such as the fear of increased expectations. Like John, mentioned earlier in this chapter, maybe you don't want the burden of others expecting more from your play, or you place greater expectations on your own play. Maybe you think that being successful in golf will distract you from other career pursuits.

Top That One

One of the biggest challenges after shooting a personal-low round is to follow it up with another low round, which is similar to trying to shoot a better score than your personal-best round. Golf can be a cruel, inconsistent game. One day you are on top of the world after playing great, and the next day you can't hit a solid shot. U.S. Open winner Steve Jones said one of the biggest challenges in golf is posting another low round after shooting a career low. He, like other players, realizes that golf fortunes change every day. "It's impossible to be at the top of your game every single week. Physically you change, the courses change, conditions change, the bounces you get change, everything changes so much. To put the mind and the physical together—it has to be a combination," said Jones.

> *If we look at all the great rounds, none of them are the same, and you don't know exactly what you did, because if you did, you would shoot those scores all the time.*
>
> —HELEN ALFREDSSON

Every week you can see examples of players on the tours who shoot a low round only to follow it with a poor to mediocre round the next day. Even the pros are not immune to the problems of elevated expectations. Notah Begay is an example of a player who could not follow his career-low round with another low round. During the Nike Dominion Open, he followed up his record 59 with rounds of 74 and 74 on the weekend to finish sixth. When he shot a record 62 during the 1994 NCAA Tournament, he followed it up with rounds of 73 and 73 and finished sixth that week also. He reasoned that he shot 74-74 on the weekend because his game was inconsistent from one day to the next. For him, playing well has a lot to do with attitude, feeling the rhythm, rolling putts in, and getting good breaks. These variables change from day to day.

One reason why it's so hard to follow up a personal-best round with another low round is that you compare every round played to your personal best. The ability to shoot low scores flows from good putting, proper thoughts and attitude, hitting the ball well enough to score, and getting a few fortunate breaks. Every subsequent round is then compared to how well you were playing when you shot your low round. Golf doesn't feel as easy as before, when the shots seemed effortless. It's easy to become impatient, because the putts are not dropping as they did when you were putting well. You don't get the "good bounces" you did when you shot your personal best. In addition, your elevated expectations cause you to become frustrated with your lack of immediate results.

Thinking Beyond the Box

To perform to your full potential, you must change how you usually think about your golf game and how you perceive yourself. You must understand and overcome the barriers that impede your performance. Your point of view of the world around you and of yourself needs to change. In short, you must play beyond "the box."

People in the business world coined the term "thinking beyond the box" to describe the type of thinking that is needed to tackle tough problems and to generate innovative ideas and strategies. Social conditioning and predictable approaches to problems in the business world produce comfort zones that stifle creative thinking. By encouraging employees to think outside the box, businesses seek to move them out of comfort zones and predictable thought processes to make breakthroughs in creativity. The ability to think, solve problems creatively, and generate new ideas is what determines the success of many businesses in today's world of ever-evolving technology and social trends.

To achieve greater golfing success and continue to shoot low scores, you also have to learn how to think beyond the box and move outside of your comfort zones. Thinking beyond the box starts with identifying the barriers to success that hold you back from shooting lower scores. It also means looking at your game from another perspective, thinking differently about how you play, and changing old habits of thinking and behavior. Let's examine a few ways you can play outside the box after shooting a personal-low round.

Change Your Scoring Self-Image

Often the labels we give ourselves become limiting beliefs. Examples of ways we use labels include "I'm an average putter," "I'm an OK player," or "I always shoot in the 90s." These labels form your golfing self-image. Once you break an important scoring milestone (90, 80, 70, etc.), a new scoring self-image has to form. Just breaking 90 once will not help you form a new self-image. To continue to shoot in the 80s, you have to accept low scores as the norm and not the exception. This means you have to believe on any day that you can score in the 80s. Otherwise, the label "I always shoot in the 90s" will limit your ability to continue to break 90 repeatedly.

How do you progress from the self-image of "I shoot in the 90s" to "I shoot in the 80s"? The first option is to visualize yourself shooting the scores you are capable of shooting. By doing this you begin to internalize the idea that you can continue to break 90. Another option is to keep your self-talk in line with what you want to achieve. Begin by recognizing your own self-talk, especially self-talk that limits your ability. Instead of saying to yourself, "I'm not a good enough putter to shoot low scores," you might want to replace that statement with "I'm a good putter and I continue to improve every day." You can easily ignore comments others make about your game, but it's difficult to ignore your own internal dialogue. Make sure it is positive and self-empowering.

Reward Yourself for Your Success

Persons who disqualify their achievements and don't reward themselves or accept compliments are at risk for low self-confidence. You have to step back and think outside the box about your performance. Don't make excuses and attribute a low score to luck or an easy course. You should take pride in your accomplishment. Review each round and replay the good shots you hit and the putts you made to break 90, 80, or 70 for the first time. Most golfers are quick to be judgmental and look back on the round and say, "If only I had not missed those two short putts or hit that ball in the water. What a round it could have been." Golfers have a propensity to first recall what they did wrong, how they messed up, or the mistakes that cost them shots during the round.

Start by recalling what you did well first. Instead of berating yourself for what you did wrong, ask yourself what you did well after each shot, putt, or chip. Second, always review the round with rose-colored glasses. Don't be self-critical and focus only on what you did wrong. Acknowledge what you did well on each hole. Go ahead and examine your weaknesses objectively to help you improve as a golfer, not as a way to scold yourself and ruin your self-confidence. Third, do something positive for yourself when you play a good round or shoot your personal-best score. Buy a gift for yourself, take some time off, or reward yourself by playing a golf course you always wanted to play.

Post Lower Scores

Tour pros are used to shooting low scores because they play and practice every day. You might not be able to play or practice every day, but you can get used to shooting lower scores. Recently, I received a telephone call from a father who was concerned about his 15-year-old son's golf game. His son was starting to shoot in the high 60s to low 70s from the up tees. He asked me if it was a good idea to have his son play from the back tees at his home course to make the game more challenging. Based on what I know about comfort zones, I suggested that he not move his son to the back tees. I would prefer him to get used to shooting low numbers on the up tees instead of struggling to make par on the back tees. I encouraged the father to help his son adopt a mentality that he can take it deep on any given day. When he got longer, then he could play from the back tees.

This is what helped Doug Dunakey shoot 59 on the Nike Tour. He told me that growing up and playing on an easy home course helped him get used to posting low scores. He said, "I'm used to seeing low numbers because of the course I grew up playing. The course was only 6,700 yards, and it had five par 5s. It was a good golf course, but really, 67 or 68 was par. I was used to going low. As opposed to other courses where 72 is a good score. It's a totally different mind-set."

Many players, such as Lee Janzen, pride themselves on playing the hard courses well. He always seems to play his way onto the leader board on tough courses like the U.S. Open or the Players Championship. Maybe Janzen's game is not suited to posting very low numbers on easier courses, as some other players can. Janzen is more of a grinder, a player who likes a tough challenge and loves to shoot par on difficult tracks. Other momentum players, such as John Huston, Dunakey, and Begay, rely on making birdies to get into the rhythm of play. The momentum sparks their confidence or rhythm, and they can go low.

Whatever tees you play from, you can use Dunakey's strategy to make a scoring breakthrough. Play a few rounds from the front tees, or if you already play from the front tees, try playing two balls off the tee or into the greens. The idea is not to teach you to cheat, but to get you used to shooting lower scores, thus changing your scoring self-concept. Even though you are playing a shorter course, you still have to hit shots and make putts. The goal is to record fewer bogeys and more pars on the scorecard with some birdies mixed in. After you get comfortable breaking 90 (or 80) from the up tees or playing two balls at a time, move back to your regular tees and play only one ball. Hopefully your scoring self-concept will change to that of an 80s player while you post lower scores.

Set Higher Goals

Do you set yourself up for underachievement by setting goals that are not challenging or difficult? Do you accept mediocre golf? Do you make excuses for why you won't play well before you even start the round? Undermotivated golfers lack the appropriate level of drive to play their best golf. Even golfers who are highly motivated may sell themselves short with goals that are too easy to attain. A big challenge in golf is to set goals (remember, goals are not the same as expectations) that are challenging and difficult enough to push you, but realistic enough that you can achieve them. If you carry a 16-handicap, it may be wishful thinking to be an 8 by the end of the golf season, but you may be able to set a goal of getting to a 13 or 14. This is still a lofty goal, but one that may be very possible.

I prefer you set goals that will help lead to good scores instead of focusing on score. Let me explain. You already know I am not a fan of target scores, because target scores can limit your performance. Nevertheless, I am a fan of goals that help you achieve low scores. For example, if you are trying to shoot in the 80s more consistently, you should set goals that will help you do just that. What type of goals do you need to set to shoot in the 80s? I would start by calculating how many fairways and greens you hit on average when you play. Then you can calculate how many fairways and greens you need to hit to shoot lower scores.

Let's say you usually hit about six greens in regulation and eight fairways per round when you score in the 90s. In order to shoot more consistently in the 80s, hitting eight greens and nine fairways per round will give you a better chance. Using this method, you can set your goals based on how many greens and fairways you need to hit to shoot in the 80s more consistently. You can set goals for any part of your game, including number of fairways, greens, total putts, up-and-down percentage, sand saves, birdie opportunities, and reducing the number of three-putts per round. This can be applied to any level golf you play; just adjust the statistics you need to break your scoring milestone.

You can choose many statistics in golf, but don't go crazy here and have too many goals. Pick two or three goals that are critical to your score improvement. For example, if missing fairways is a weakness that prevents you from shooting better scores, you may want to focus on hitting more fairways per round. If you are three-putting two or more times per round, you should work on decreasing the number of three-putts per round to zero. Decide on what areas of your game you need to improve that will have the biggest impact on scoring. Then develop goals to improve those areas of your game and bring them more in line with your strengths.

Acknowledge Your Fears

To get beyond the fear of success or failure, you need to recognize that you have fears and how these fears prevent you from reaching your golfing potential. I've discussed fear of success and the potential problems that it may bring to a golfer. Players sabotage their own performance because they want to avoid the problems that are associated with newfound success. Fear of failure can also derail golfers from shooting low scores, because it causes players to try too hard, overthink each shot, and stifle their performance with anxiety.

If you play golf for fun, you don't have to worry about these fears, but if you want to shoot lower scores and win tournaments, you have to face them head-on. You might ask yourself, What's the worst thing that can happen to me when I fail at golf? or What problems do I foresee if I shoot a personal-best round? Once you identify and acknowledge your fears, it is much easier to overcome them.

Final Thoughts

It is very gratifying to score a career round and break a personal scoring milestone (100, 90, 80, par, 70). For one day, you got the most out of your round, got a few friendly bounces, and scored your best. To continue to make progress, it's important to break out of old habits of thinking, set new goals, and continue to shoot low scores. The first step is to identify stagnant beliefs and learn to think outside the box. Start by recognizing and abolishing the subtle forms of self-sabotage and expectations that hinder your ability to perform. To shoot lower scores, it's important to recognize your ability, reward yourself for your achievement, and believe you can shoot more low scores.

Every player's game changes from day to day. Many variables impact performance, including course conditions, weather conditions, luck, and how you think, feel, and act on the golf course. Avoid comparing every round played to your personal-best round. Comparisons only set the foundation for frustration. Continue to improve each part of your game, identifying your weaknesses, improving them, and building your strengths. On the golf course, set aside your preconceived notions about what is and is not possible to achieve and focus on playing your best one shot at a time. The next time you are in the zone or feel the rhythm, embrace the feeling and ride it all the way to the clubhouse.

Breaking Your Personal Scoring Milestone

You're supposed to continue to try and get better. That doesn't mean that you're going to get better, but I'm trying to get better. I'm trying to work on every facet of my game.

—TIGER WOODS (CAREER LOW: 61)

Every golfer who begins playing starts out as a "hacker" and hopes only to hit the ball on the clubface when he swings. For new players, breaking 100 is out of the question. The golf swing feels too unnatural, to say the least. Learning the rules of the game is mind-boggling. Getting a grip on course etiquette is a task in itself. Most beginners go through stages of missing the ball altogether to digging a six-foot divot with every swing to hitting line-drive iron shots. Golf is not an easy game to learn. The frustration associated with mastering the game has caused many potentially good golfers to quit. However, after one learns the basics of golf, attention can shift to other challenges of the game and how to play better and score well.

Once hooked on the game, golfers have an urge to play better and continuously shoot lower scores. After breaking 100 for the first time, the next goal is to break 90, then 80, and so forth. It's a never-ending journey to see how you can improve your game. *Going Low* is about helping you shoot lower scores repetitively and surpassing scoring milestones. Until now, this book has discussed the psychological factors influencing the ability to shoot a low round. You learned about how personal barriers and expectations limit behavior and have come to realize the mental hazards of comfort zones in golf and how to overcome them.

The goal of this chapter is to summarize and link together specific mental keys to help both high- and low-handicap golfers score a personal-best round. It draws on previous chapters to show you how to mentally approach a round of golf, from start to finish. This chapter is divided into two sections. The first section discusses tips for 90 to 100-plus players, and the second is for 70 to 80-plus players.

Breaking 100 or 90 for the First Time

Every fledgling golfer would love to play well enough to break 100. This feat is not easy even for the most talented newcomer. Very few golfers can pick up a set of clubs and break 100 (under the rules of the game) the first time out without any formal instruction or structured on-range practice.

If you shoot in the 90s to over 100, more than likely you are an inconsistent golfer both from shot to shot and from day to day. You can't consistently hit the ball on the center of the clubface every time or hit the center of the fairway. You may make solid contact one or two times out of each 10 shots hit, whereas a low-handicap golfer may make solid contact seven or eight times out of 10 shots. Even the pros don't hit every shot solid. The strategic and mental sides of the game are foreign, because you spend most of the time mastering the fundamental skills. If your goal is to break 100 or 90 for the first time, this section will address your attitude on the way to the course; what to do in the warm-up; the first-tee process; and the first holes, middle holes, and final holes of the round; it will also give you practice tips to help you reach your goal of breaking a scoring milestone.

On the Way to the Course

Enjoy the ride to the course! Don't stress about your performance. Most important, don't worry about embarrassing yourself if you shoot a high number that day. Many golfers are too conscious of embarrassment. The fear of embarrassment will affect your performance, as you will play scared and tight to avoid shooting a bad round. This mind-set will not help you succeed. You are not a pro golfer and you don't play golf for a living. Golf should be fun, not a grueling test of your pride and ego.

The best option is to set a goal to have fun and enjoy your day with friends or colleagues. Very competitive golfers let their pride get in the way of having fun on the golf course, because they are too consumed with winning. Remind yourself why you like to play golf. Don't forget to relish the good shots and reward yourself often. Take pride that practice and many rounds of golf are paying dividends in and of themselves.

Make sure you prompt yourself to relax if you hit a bad shot. Learn to be proficient at handling bad shots. It's best if you have a very short memory for a bad shot; don't carry one bad past shot to the next. If you do, the anger and frustration will make you overcompensate, and you'll swing faster or be so mad that you can't see the ball in front of you. Not only will these things damage your focus, but you also won't enjoy the round.

If you are the type of player who gets upset after hitting a poor shot, here's what I suggest: before the start of the round, give yourself the equivalent of 10 "get-out-of-the-doghouse" cards to use after a bad shot (symbolic or literal cards). Everyone hits bad shots, some more than others. Hitting a bad shot won't ruin the round unless your attitude causes you to not enjoy the round. What's important is how you respond to hitting a bad shot. Anger, frustration, and despair will ruin both your score and your day. Give yourself the luxury of hitting 10 poor shots. This way you can easily play on with composure after a mistake. Your primary goal should be to stay calm and relaxed after you have a bad hole or hit a couple of bad shots in a row.

Warming Up

For the 90 to 100-plus shooter who wants to break 90 or 100 for the first time: Do not skip the warm-up. The purpose of the warm-up is to get loose and prepare for the day's round. It's also a transition between other activities in life and golf. Good players get their game face on and get focused for golf during this time.

Don't neglect a full warm-up routine. If you do, the first few holes will be your warm-up, and that doesn't help you score your best. It takes a few swings to get into a groove and work the kinks out of your swing. A poor start with a couple of double bogeys can give you a bad attitude for the rest of the round. To get off to a good start, it's important to take enough time to get loose, gain some confidence with a few solid shots, and warm up your putting.

If you have only a few minutes before tee time, make sure you stretch the major muscle groups (such as your legs, back, chest, and shoulders) used in golf, hit a few long putts, and take some full practice swings to loosen your body in preparation for play. Above all else, get a feel for the speed of the greens by hitting several long putts. Most poor putting is caused by a lack of speed control. The goal is to eliminate three- and four-putts, which are killers to shooting low scores.

First Tee Shot

A tee shot is tough enough, but it is even more difficult when this is your first shot of the day and you think everyone in the clubhouse is watching. The first tee shot can often make or break a round, because it sets up your performance on the first hole. First-tee jitters can turn a straightforward shot into the most difficult shot you'll hit all day.

You may have experienced two different types of first-tee jitters. The first is the friendly kind of butterflies characterized by excitement and anticipation. This is a good feeling of anticipation of the start of the round. You feel excited to play and ready to get going. These butterflies can help you play better by getting you focused. You are excited, your heart is pounding faster, and your focus becomes more acute. The pros often experience this type of butterflies and interpret them as necessary for playing well.

The second kind of first-tee jitters is the type that make you have a sinking feeling in the pit of your gut. Your mind races, your heart rate accelerates, your palms sweat, your muscles tighten, your blood pressure increases, and you get an uncomfortable feeling in your stomach. If you feel anxious or afraid, your performance suffers, because it makes you physically tense and cripples your ability to focus. A golfer feels this when he or she is afraid to hit a bad shot or embarrass him- or herself, or is afraid of losing the match on the first hole. Once you experience "bad" jitters, you become obsessed with the uncomfortable feelings, which distract you from what you need to focus on.

The first kind of jitters is helpful to your performance, but the second can be detrimental to your game. If you experience "bad" jitters, the first step is to address your fears. What are the possible fears a player might undergo before hitting the first tee shot?

- Fear of embarrassment—don't want to look stupid in front of others.
- Fear of hitting a bad shot—don't want to get off to a bad start.
- Fear of losing the match—afraid to lose the game to a rival.
- Fear of not playing up to your own expectations—tired of the frustration from not achieving up to your abilities.
- Fear of not being respected as a golfer—worry about how others will perceive you as a person and golfer.

As you can tell, most fears about the first tee shot come from worry about what other people think about you or your concerns about playing poorly. I would prefer that you adopt a more rational philosophy to dispute your own, often irrational, fears. For example, tackle your own fears by telling yourself that one shot is not going to make others judge you or your golf game. What's the worst thing that can happen if you hit a bad shot in front of a friend? A true friend will still be one regardless of your hitting one poor tee shot.

Try to put your fears aside and focus on something more pleasant. Keep your mind distracted from the first tee shot until it's your turn to hit. Relax and talk with your playing buddies before it's the group's time to tee off. When you're up, take as many practice swings as needed until you get the feeling of a relaxed swing before you address the ball. Then try to reproduce that feeling over the ball. Take your time and don't hurry the first tee shot to "get it over with." This will only make you swing harder. Remember to aim at a specific target in the fairway, rather than aim at the fairway. Pace yourself by walking up to the ball with the confidence that you can make solid contact, and nothing more.

Opening Holes

For many golfers, the opening holes set the tone for the rest of the round. A golfer's confidence is often dictated by how well he or she plays the first few holes. This can be a problem after a poor start. If you get off to a good start to a round and hit a few quality shots, your confidence soars and carries you for several holes. If you get off to a poor start to a round, any confidence you had starting the round is gone and you will struggle for the remainder of the round.

Let's say you get off to a good start to the round and shoot par, bogey, bogey on the first three holes. Hopefully, you have some momentum, confidence, and feel for your game. But many holes still remain. You don't want to become too giddy with a good start to the round—it may blow up in your face if you have a bad hole. Stay levelheaded with your emotions if you have a good or poor start.

Some golfers turn pessimistic when they are playing better than expected and start to sabotage their performance by thinking the start is too good to be true. "OK, when am I going to make my first triple bogey," a player might say to herself or jokingly comment to her playing partners. Recognize self-sabotaging comments or thoughts as a comfort zone problem. Don't automatically assume that you are destined for a big screwup after a great start, as this will only become a self-fulfilling prophecy. By implanting pessimistic thoughts in your mind, you start to look for holes where you may make a high number, causing you to play defensively.

Middle Holes

The middle holes are important to keeping a good round going. This is when you have to put the score on the back burner and try to have fun on the golf course. Relax between shots by talking with your playing partners and enjoying the golf course setting. After 12 holes or so, you could start to run out of energy. Many golfers make the mistake of grinding too hard between shots and thinking about their next shot before it's time to play it. This taxes concentration for the later holes. Relaxing between shots reserves your energy to focus on the final stretch of holes.

If you have a personal-best round going and you know it, don't get too excited about shooting a good score or discouraged about shooting a poor score. You want to play on an even emotional keel.

Trying to keep a good round going over 18 holes (four to five hours) can place too much pressure on you. Instead, break up the round into segments, such as three groups of six holes or six groups of three holes. Treat each segment mentally as if it is an individual round. Once you complete a segment (or mini-round) of six holes, for example, forget about what you did on those holes and start fresh with the next segment. This way you can put your score for the first six holes behind you and focus only on the next six holes.

Knowing you scored well on the first six holes might cause you to start thinking about your final score: "I'm only six over par for the first six holes; I can easily break 100 today." This thinking is not advised when you have a good round going. You can set simple goals for each of the six holes, such as hitting two fairways and two greens in regulation. A reasonable goal is to keep the ball in play for all six holes. High-handicap players lose many strokes by hitting the ball out of play, adding costly penalty shots to the score. You don't have to play heroic golf. Playing smart golf is very important to scoring your best. No matter what level player you are, selecting proper clubs and targets to keep the ball in play is always a good idea. This means you might hit an iron off the tee to put the ball in the fairway. Instead of trying to be a hero and carry the water on your second shot into a par 4, you might decide to lay up short of the water and hit your third shot onto the green.

Final Holes

You made it to the 16th tee with a chance to break 100 for the first time. How do you keep a good round going and finish strong? The best scenario is that you aren't aware of your score and don't know you have a chance to break 100. Like most golfers, however, you probably write down the score (or mentally note it) after each hole and add it up as you play, knowing exactly where you stand. You realize that breaking 100 is possible if you make double bogey or better on each of the remaining holes.

The last thing you want to do is think about your score on the final three holes and what you need to shoot on each hole to break 100. Thinking about the score you may potentially shoot only creates tension. Instead, the goal is to hit quality shots and keep the ball in play. How you plan each shot is critical to a strong finish. Use whatever club you can to get the ball into the fairway. It's fine to hit an iron off the tee on a tight hole or a hole with water adjacent to the fairway. You may want to consider playing conservatively on par-3 holes that are dangerously close to the water, out of bounds, or near trees by laying up your first shot. Instead of trying to kill a 3-wood to advance the ball down a par-5 fairway, it might be wise to select an iron or a 7-wood to play down the center of the fairway. The goal is to score your best, not try to hit perfect shots.

Practice Goals

To break your personal scoring milestone consistently, you need to develop some practice goals. Your game will improve if you play a couple of rounds a week without formal practice, but it will improve faster if you set some time aside to work on the consistency of your swing and putting stroke. Here are some suggestions:

- Set a goal to practice your game at least a few hours per week. Separate your practice into long game, short game, and putting practice. Whatever the time you have to practice, divide your total practice time by three to cover all areas of the game.

Remember that putting and chipping account for more than 50 percent of your score.

- Work on controlling how far you can hit each putt. Three- and four-putting are main culprits that prevent you from scoring lower. Both are speed-control or touch problems. Spend one hour or more each week lagging the ball close to the hole from long range (30, 40, 50, and 60 feet).

- Schedule a lesson with a pro at least once a month to work on your swing and putting mechanics. You want to be able to practice correctly when you do spend the time, so make sure you are working on the correct method before you devote more time to practice. (Refer to my book *Peak Performance Golf* for advice on how to improve practice and get the most out of your golf lessons.)

- Visualize how you want your swing to look and feel. Use a model player who has a build similar to yours and watch that player swing. The more you can visualize what a good swing looks and feels like, the easier it will be to make the appropriate changes. (My game often improves when I go to a tournament and watch players hit balls on the range. I get a clearer mental picture of the proper golf swing and am able to visualize the swing later on.)

Breaking 80 or 70 for the First Time

Unlike the 90 to 100-plus player, your game is more consistent from shot to shot and day to day. Although the 70-plus golfer is a better player, he is faced with the same challenges as his counterpart who shoots in the 80s. Eliminating the effect of a comfort zone at both levels of the game is equally important. In this section, I'll discuss tips for breaking 80 and other milestones for the first time. I'll be your instructor from driving to the course to finishing off a good round. You'll learn the proper attitude and thoughts you need during the first, middle, and final holes of the round to help you score well and record a personal-best round.

On the Way to the Course

Before leaving for the course, check to make sure you have all your clubs in the bag, enough balls for the day, and rain gear if the weather starts to get nasty. It's better to be overprepared than underprepared. Take an extra golf glove and towel with you in the event that you need to stay dry. Bring some snacks to munch on after the turn to keep your energy high for the last few holes.

As you commute to the course, go over your game plan for the day. You want to set up a strategy before you get on the first tee; you'll make better decisions now than you will in the midst of a low round. Your game plan should include what clubs you will hit off each tee, smart targets to aim to, and what par-5 holes you will lay up on or go for in two shots. Remind yourself to stick to your game plan, and don't let overexcitement during the round (or despair from a poor one) make you alter the game plan. Keep in mind that with the exception of the course layout and weather conditions, you need to follow your game plan as closely as possible.

Play or sing a favorite song to get in a good state of mind before arriving at the golf course. Play one of your favorite albums that is both inspirational and relaxing. I wouldn't suggest any heavy-metal or other intense music at this time. You don't want to get too hyped up before you get to the golf course.

Drain your mind of expectations. No one plays ideal golf or hits perfect shots when they play. Golf is a game of misses. You don't have to hit the ball perfectly to score your best, either. Release the idea of shooting a specific score for the day. As discussed earlier, a target score will only limit your success, especially when you are in the midst of a good round. Don't take *any* expectations (putting, ball-striking, etc.) into the round, for that matter. Instead, be confident that you can execute each shot as planned. Instead of setting a target score, set goals for how many greens and fairways to hit. Decide how many greens and fairways you need to hit to break 80 or break 70. How many greens and fairways did you hit when you shot your lowest score? Maybe you hit seven fairways and eight greens to shoot 81. If so, then set a goal to hit eight fairways and 10 greens for the round. Remember, you strive for goals; it's OK if you don't reach your goals every day.

Warming Up

You should already have a set warm-up routine to use before you play a round. If you don't, you had best develop one. A good warm-up routine can help you to make the transition between other activities in your life and golf.

In addition to your normal warm-up routine, hit a few shots with the clubs you might use on the opening holes of the golf course. Visualize the golf hole on the range and pretend you are hitting your first tee shot or approach shot into the first green. Use your entire mental preshot routine, just as you do physically on the course. Tighten your mind on the target.

It would be an error to focus on swing mechanics at this time. It's too late to make any swing changes. Find one or maybe two swing cues on the range to take to the course, preferably related to the tempo, balance, or rhythm of your golf swing. The best option is to think about only the target as you swing, letting the body react to the input of the target.

If you have a good warm-up, take that confidence with you to the first tee. If you don't feel good about the warm-up, don't panic. Many golfers hit the ball better on the course. Know that you will focus better once you're on the course. The goal is to get into a confident state of mind, have no expectations about outcomes, and prepare to focus on one shot at a time. Don't forget to warm up your mind by hitting five shots with your full preshot routine.

Also, spend some time with a putting warm-up. The most important thing you can do to prepare yourself is to get a feel for the speed of the greens by hitting a few short putts into the center of the cup to see success. If you have only 15 minutes before the round to warm up, make sure you hit some long putts to get a feel for the speed of the greens. Stretch out and take a few practice swings before the first tee shot.

First Tee Shot

As an experienced golfer, you know that the first tee shot sets the tone for the entire round. Any first-tee jitters will dissipate soon after you hit the first tee shot. Help the butterflies in your stomach to fly in formation. As discussed earlier, two different types of first-tee jitters exist: friendly butterflies and unfriendly jitters. A player can interpret first-tee jitters in two ways: as helpful and friendly, or as unhelpful and undesirable.

Know that first-tee nerves are part of golf. Interpret them as a way of getting you focused for the first tee shot and giving you the rush of adrenaline you need. This is how the pros look at first-tee nerves. Focusing too much on the uncomfortable feelings only heightens the tension. Don't bring more attention to the knot in your stomach or your rapid heartbeat when you feel the unfriendly jitters. Shift your attention to your game plan and how you should play the first hole.

You have several options to prepare yourself for the first tee shot. Use what works best for you:

- Visualize the shot you want to hit. Feel a smooth swing as you take a couple practice swings and visualize the ball flying to your target. This helps instill confidence and focuses you on execution instead of "What if I top my first-tee ball?"

- Relax and talk with your playing partners. Take your mind off the first tee shot. Some players work themselves into a state of anxiety as they stand around and do nothing while waiting to hit their first shot. Keep your mind occupied with other thoughts. When it's your turn to hit, don't rush your routine. Take your time to go through the routine and visualize a good shot.

- Reconfirm your goals for the day to help you focus on the process. Write down your goals on your scorecard or on something you can see. I've created cue cards for tour players I've worked with as a reminder to focus on their goals for the day. They keep the goals in their yardage book, and every time they open it, the cue card "focus on the process" is directly in sight as a reminder.

- If you are a person who gets too anxious to pull the trigger, try some simple relaxation exercises before it's your turn to hit. Take a few deep breaths through the abdominal region. As you inhale, shrug your shoulders to your ears. As you exhale, drop your shoulders and release the tension. Tighten and release your grip on the club to prevent the "death grip." You want to release the tension in your hands, arms, and shoulders before you address the ball.

- Last, focus on execution and hitting the fairway. You can't make birdie (or bogey) on the first shot. Ask yourself, "What do I need to do to hit a good shot?" The answer will provide you with the appropriate task-relevant cues. Pick your target, see the shot you want to hit, feel the shot with a practice swing, aim and align, and focus on your target.

If you begin to worry about embarrassing yourself or hitting a poor shot, stop and restart the routine from the beginning. You don't have to hit a shot until you are ready to do so. Use this time to get refocused on your routine. You are not ready to hit the shot if you are thinking about who is watching you hit, what the bet is for the day, or how to avoid hitting the ball into the trees. Anytime during the round, if you are not into your preshot routine, stop and get refocused on the task.

Opening Holes

It's key to get off to a solid start to the round, because the opening holes often dictate the momentum and confidence for the rest of the round, as discussed in Chapter 2. If you get off to a good start to the round and par the first four holes, your confidence can soar and carry you the rest of the round. After a poor start, a player with frail confidence will lose momentum and suffer the rest of the round.

If you start the round off with a bang and make par, par, birdie, par on the first four holes, the goal is to continue to play well. It's too early to even think about breaking 70 (or 80) at this point in the round. A comfort zone should not affect your play. You still have a lot of holes to play, so it shouldn't cross your mind. Keep focused on the present shot and don't look back.

Some golfers may get overconfident in this situation. Don't let your performance on the first few holes go to your head. Overconfidence can cause you to try low-percentage shots and play too aggressively in some situations. Stick to the game plan even though every part of your game is working and you feel like you have the confidence of Tiger Woods. Be aggressive when you have a good chance to go for birdie, but also play smart golf when it is called for.

If you don't play well on the opening holes, you have to do everything in your power to stay confident and create momentum. Some of the lowest rounds shot on tour started slowly. When Ted Tryba shot 61 at the 1999 Los Angeles Open, he was even par after five holes with one bogey and only one birdie. When Notah Begay shot 59 in the 1998 Nike Dominion Open, he was only two under through seven holes. Most of the fireworks happened on the back nine for both players. When David Duval shot his career-low 59, he birdied holes 14, 15, and 16 and eagled 18. Without such a strong finish he would not have shot 59 that day.

Sometimes an average or mediocre start can be an advantage as long as the player keeps his or her head in the game and remains patient. Golfers who get off to a strong start on the front nine can become score conscious early in the round and protect their score. This happens when the 80-plus golfer shoots 39 on the front nine only to follow it up with a 43 on the back. If you think too far ahead about your potential score, your comfort zone makes you back up on the final holes.

Compare this attitude to that of a pitcher throwing a no-hitter in baseball. If a pitcher is throwing a no-hitter in the first few innings, he doesn't feel any pressure yet. It's too early in the game to be burdened by the possibility of a no-hitter. As the game progresses, the pressure to throw a no-hitter mounts. Into the seventh inning and beyond, it's harder to just focus on the task and forget about the no-hitter—everyone on the field is aware of it! But in order to throw the no-hitter, the pitcher needs to stay focused on one pitch at a time.

Unlike throwing a no-hitter, the pressure to shoot your lowest round ever can start early in golf, after nine holes. However, you could get off to an average start and be playing an average round for 12 holes, and then all of a sudden your game comes alive. You make a few pars or a couple of birdies on the final holes. Before you realize just how well you were playing, the round is over. A comfort zone never had an opportunity to affect your performance. A late flurry of pars for the 80-plus player or a couple birdies for the 70-plus player can turn an average round into a great round without enough time to notice you are on fire and going low. This is often how golfers shoot their career-low rounds.

If you don't have momentum early, it's important to not lose your composure or confidence. You never know what can happen on the back nine. My low round in Florida came when I shot an ugly 44 on the front and a career-low 32 on the back nine. Your game can turn around fast if you keep composed and wait for it to happen. Sometimes when a golfer is stuck in neutral and has no momentum, he or she can sabotage the round by thinking, "I'm playing poorly today, nothing is happening." It's not that you're playing poorly; you just have not had anything good happen in the round.

Remember, "good" is a relative term. For a tour pro, good means making a birdie or two. For an 80-plus player, good means making a few solid pars or a great par save. Your negative attitude can prevent you from catching a wave of momentum and turn around the round.

Momentum can turn on a dime as long as you stay composed and wait for good things to happen. Look for signs that your game is about to change for the positive. Holing a long putt, making a great save, hitting a perfect drive down the center of the fairway, or getting a good break can be interpreted as a sign that your game is about to come alive. If your game is stuck in neutral, look for reasons to catch a wave of momentum and grow your confidence.

Middle Holes

During the middle of the round, some golfers tend to "go to sleep" and not focus as well. Research on human behavior tells us that we are more likely to remember the beginning and the end of a task or event. Think about the last time you read a book or watched a movie. The odds are that you can remember the beginning and the end, but do you remember much that happened in the middle? Maybe this explains the tendency for some golfers to drift off during the middle holes.

If you are playing well, it's more likely that you are alert during the middle holes of the round. If you are not playing well, you may lose interest in the round, which explains the loss of focus during the middle holes. Whatever the situation, to keep a good round alive, you have to stay focused during the middle holes. Remind yourself what your goals are for the round and recommit to your game plan for the middle holes. Use your focus during the preshot routine as an indication of your level of focus.

If you do shoot 39 (for the 80-plus player) or 34 (for the 70-plus player) on the front nine and are in position to break 80 or 70, how do you keep the good round going?

1. Don't add up your score for the front nine. You know you are playing well; you don't need to confirm it by looking at the scorecard. Ask someone else to keep your score for you.

2. Forget about the last nine and what you shot. It's a new nine holes and you start at even par again.

3. Stick to your game plan that you set up before the round started. You don't want to become too aggressive or too conservative now.

4. Challenge yourself to play aggressive but smart golf. When you know you are playing well, the tendency is to protect the score. Stay focused on where you want to hit the ball instead of where you don't want to hit the ball. Make sure your last look (over the ball) is to your target and not the water or tree line.

5. Break the remaining nine holes into three-hole stretches. This will make the last nine holes less complicated. Set goals for what you want to do on each three-hole segment.

Final Holes

With a strong finish on the last four holes, you have a chance to break 70 for the first time. Many golfers lose track of their score when playing in the zone. They are so focused on playing golf, one shot at a time, that they don't pay attention to score. Mentally, this is the best scenario for a golfer to complete the round. One exception, though: if you are trying to win a tournament, you may need to know where you stand on the last two holes and what you need to do to win.

> *When you're really playing that well, you don't realize the score. You're in the golf shot, but the sense of past or future doesn't exist. You're right here, so you don't really know.*
>
> —HELEN ALFREDSSON

If you are like most golfers, you are a good mathematician and know exactly what the score is after 14 holes. This becomes a problem if you start to calculate what you need to shoot on the final four holes to break 80. "I'm six over par now; if I make three pars and one bogey on the final holes, I can shoot 79!" Stop right there! Don't set yourself up for failure by projecting your final score. Thinking about your final score won't help you hit the shot you are currently hitting. A focus on score is only a distraction that makes you nervous. In order to score well on the last four holes, stay focused on playing golf and what you need to do to hit quality shots. If you start to think ahead, catch yourself immediately and refocus on the next shot.

This technique is called the "Three R's": recognize—regroup—refocus. The first step to changing behavior is to recognize faulty thinking. Here you recognize that you are thinking about future holes ("Gee, what do I need to shoot on the final holes to break 80?"). The next step is to interrupt the faulty thinking. Regroup by distracting yourself ("Stop thinking about your score! That won't help you focus on the process."). The last step is to refocus on the task in front of you. You can do this by asking yourself a simple question: "What do I need to focus on to hit a good shot right now?"

Instead of trying to avoid making one or more bogeys on the final holes, challenge yourself to be aggressive (while still playing within yourself), to put yourself in position to make a birdie or solid par. The goal should be to have more "birdie opportunities" instead of avoiding bogeys. If you try not to make bogeys, what usually happens to your game? You find a way to make bogeys by playing too safe or cautious. Set a goal such as getting three birdie opportunities on the final four holes. (I define a birdie opportunity as a birdie putt within 25 feet of the hole.) Another goal could be a short, straightforward chip for birdie. When you start using goals instead of thinking about shots to avoid, you focus on success—and if you fall short you still can make a par on each hole.

I think it's also important to have a shot you can rely on—a "go-to shot." When the pressure is on and you want to get the ball in the fairway, you need a specific shot you can rely on almost every time. A low round is a low round even if it is ugly. The go-to shot may be a low cut, a low punch shot, or a big hook. Use whatever type of shot you can produce most consistently under pressure. Scoring well is all about getting the job done, not playing picture-perfect shots!

I've always been a big believer of getting the ball in play and keeping it in play, whatever it takes.
—Tiger Woods

Take advantage of your good play and make it work for you instead of against you. Allow your scoring confidence to carry you to the end of the round. Keep momentum on your side by ignoring bad breaks, brushing off a bad shot quickly, and staying patient with your putting. I've seen players derail a good round after missing short birdie putts. So don't let one shot wipe out the momentum and confidence you have built up the entire round!

Practice Goals

To successfully break your personal scoring barrier and shoot lower scores repeatedly, you should work on the scoring areas of your game. The goal should be to practice the scoring shots: putting, chipping, wedge play, bunker shots, and specialty shots. Everyone wants to hit the perfect-looking drive down the center of the fairway, but improving your short game will lead to lower scoring faster.

- Set a goal to spend 75 percent of your practice working on scoring shots. A good chip or putt to help you save par will keep momentum on your side and a good round going.

- If you are three-putting one or more times a round, set a time aside to work on your touch. Most three-putts result from poor distance control (touch). Hit a lot of long putts from various distances. (Refer to my book *Peak Performance Golf* for drills to improve touch.)

- Use course management to your advantage. This will help you get the most out of your strengths as a golfer. Read what the pros do to prepare for a round. Watch a pro tournament and see what they do in the practice rounds. You need to set a game plan every round you play. This consists of the clubs you will hit off the tees, target selection, when to lay up short of fairway bunkers, when to lay up on par-5 holes, and when to shoot at the center of the green. (Refer to my book *Peak Performance Golf* for course strategy procedures.)

Final Thoughts

Now you have the mental tools to help you surpass your personal scoring barrier. I've discussed how to break free of preconceptions and adopt a mentality that helps you play without the constraint of a comfort zone. While your mental game is very important to success and development as a golfer, I want to encourage you to continue to practice and improve your physical skills. You must take a multidimensional approach to your golf game when it comes to becoming a better golfer. By this I mean working on your mental game, physical game, course management, and physical fitness. Confidence alone will take your game only so far. You need a strong base of physical skills to help your confidence and improve your game.

When playing in the zone and scoring well, several variables come together to achieve peak performance. Steve Jones explained this well: "It's impossible to be at the top of your ball-striking every single week. Physically you change, the courses change, conditions change, bounces change, everything changes so much. To put the mind and the physical together—it has to be a combination."

APPENDIX
Mental Game Rx

The moment you recognize that you're playing in the zone, you are no longer in the zone.

—Patrick J. Cohn, Ph.D. (career low: 74)

The more you play golf, the more you start to realize that, much like other sports, golf is a complex game of balance between your individual talent, your mental game skill, course difficulty, and weather conditions. As I have discussed throughout *Going Low*, your ability to perform at your peak level is primarily based on the strength of your mind to overcome preconceived notions and comfort zones associated with your performance.

Over the last decade, I have devoted a great deal of time and energy to distilling information from professional and world-class golfers in order to provide real-life solutions to help you to abolish comfort zones and preconceptions so you can shoot lower scores. In *Going Low*, I have tried to include everything that I have learned from my personal experience, as well as observations from top-ranked golfers about the psychology of shooting lower scores. My hope is to provide you with the mental tools necessary to greatly enhance your overall golf performance and help you to shoot lower scores.

While I have attempted to provide solutions to the most common problems that comfort zones and mental barriers present, there are still very specific and valid questions that remain unanswered. Many of these unanswered questions may be ones that you would ask me if you had the opportunity. In this chapter, I will answer some of the questions that golfers should ask, but haven't, as well as questions from actual golfers who want solutions to their specific golfing dilemmas.

In the middle of a good round, one of my playing partners asked me why I was playing so well. This snapped me out of the zone, because I started thinking about why I was playing well. How do I keep myself in the zone when this happens?

It is common for a player to go in and out of the zone during a round of golf. Even players who often play in the zone will have trouble staying in the zone for an entire round of golf. Just knowing you are in the zone (awareness of your extraordinary play) sometimes snaps you out of the zone. If, in the middle of a round, you are trying to figure out why you are doing so well, this only pulls your energy away from the task of playing golf. Analysis can lead to paralysis in this case.

Your partner's comment could be a psych-out tactic used to disrupt your rhythm and push you out of the zone. Whether this is an intentional psych-out or not, don't let the comments of others distract you from what needs to be done. Stay focused on playing golf. You make matters worse when you start thinking about the golf swing or putting stroke and try to understand why your swing is in the slot or what you should be doing to make putts. If others compliment or comment about your game, say, "Thank you," let it pass, and get back to playing the game of golf one shot at a time. Forget about your score and why you are playing well. Refocus on your next shot.

When I have to sit on the lead of a tournament overnight, I think about not blowing the lead and tense up, and this carries over to the next day. What should I do the night before the last round of a tournament in which I am the leader?

I have included this question because an overnight lead is very similar to what a player experiences when he has a chance to score his lowest round ever. The first mistake is thinking about blowing the lead and the embarrassment you may feel if you fail. Instead, I suggest you think about playing another solid round the next day.

When Tiger Woods has a four-shot lead going into Sunday's round, he doesn't worry about messing up his chances at winning, nor does he try to protect the lead. On the front nine, the goal is to distance himself even more from the other players in the field and turn a four-shot lead into a six-shot lead. After winning the 2000 Memorial Tournament, he said, "Well, going out today, I needed to shoot a good front nine to try and increase my lead, and make sure these guys didn't have a chance on the back nine." Your mind-set should be the same. You don't want to protect a lead. This will make you think about avoiding bogeys or double bogeys. You must be playing well if you are the leader. Use your previous good play to carry confidence into the next round. Play like you want to widen your lead, but stick to the game plan.

If I am in a groove and playing well, I don't like waiting during slow play. This disrupts my rhythm. What can I do to keep the momentum of a good round when play is slow?

Slow play is a problem for faster players who get into a rhythm from shot to shot. Waiting to hit every shot can throw these players off rhythm and ruin momentum. First, adjust your pace of play to use some of the extra time you have between shots. The last thing you want to do is play "hurry-up-and-wait" golf; it makes no sense to run up to your next shot and wait for five minutes before you can hit. You might want to walk more slowly between shots, take your time getting the yardage, and plan the next shot after you get to the ball. Use the time to get prepared to hit each putt by looking at it from all sides. Second, occupy the time between shots with satisfying activities. Talk to your playing partners, observe the wildlife on the course, or bring a book or newspaper to read between shots. The worst thing you can do is lean on your golf club, stare down the group ahead of you, and complain about the slow play. Remember to focus on an enjoyable activity. The goal is to react appropriately and not let slow play frustrate you so you can maintain composure and enjoy yourself on the golf course.

I was playing the best round of my life during a match with a friend. When I started to think about winning the match, my game came unglued. Should I forget about the match and focus on shooting my best score ever?

The error you made was to start thinking about winning the match. Thinking about results (winning) caused you to play protective and scared. I would not suggest focusing on shooting your best score either. The best option is to continue to play golf without attaching outcomes to the match. Revert to the mind-set you had before you were conscious of winning the match. How did you play yourself into position to win the match? You probably played the game one shot a time, focused on each shot as if it was a round itself, and didn't add up the score as you played.

I've shot 38 on the front nine and 45 on my second nine too many times to count. I always find a way to mess up the round and play poorly on the back nine. Is there anything I can do to play better on the back?

Your situation is the prototypical example of a player who can't play beyond his comfort zone. It's very frustrating to play your best and worst golf in the same round. First, play a few rounds starting on hole number 10 instead of starting on hole number one. If it's possible, instead of playing two nines, start the round on hole 6 and play three "rounds" of six holes at a time. You have to think outside the box and view a round differently. Third, don't keep track of your score; that only makes you more score conscious. Let a playing partner keep score for you. Remember, the problem comes about when you realize how well you are playing (and become conscious of your score) on the front nine and then change your mental approach on the back nine.

I would have broken 90 many times by now if it wasn't for those double or triple bogeys I make every round. How can I avoid making a big number each round?

This is a common problem for higher-handicap players. A bad shot turns into a triple bogey and ruins their score for the round. Minimizing the damage is critical after a poor shot. First, don't get so upset after a bad shot that it causes you to try to hit a perfect recovery shot. Some players' anger makes them too aggressive on the next shot and they end up making matters worse. If you get into trouble and hit the ball into the woods, instead of trying to hit the perfect fade around and over the trees, chip out and play for bogey. Keep your emotions in check, because anger or frustration can cause you to make poor decisions on the golf course. Negative emotions also cause you to hit shots very quickly without the proper thought process.

Second, keep the ball in play. For example, if you are on a tight par 4 with water on the right and out-of-bounds on the left, you don't have to hit a driver just because everyone else hits a driver. You can play the hole like a par 5. Hit an iron off the tee, lay up with another iron, and wedge the ball on for a chance to make par, at worst bogey. It's a lot easier to play from the fairway than from the bottom of the lake! Third, don't carry the expectation that you will make a big number at some point during the round. That expectation may turn into reality with your help.

There is this one hole at my golf course that always kills me. I make a double bogey or worse on the hole every time I play it, and this spoils my round. How do I get past my mental block on this golf hole?

I get this question often. The problem starts with your preconceptions of what's a good score on the hole. Based on experience, you think this particular hole is "out to get you" and that you can't perform well on the hole. This becomes a generalization, such as "I always score high on this hole no matter what I do." This generalization may turn into a self-fulfilling prophecy. When you approach the tee box, you are already defensive: "How will I avoid making a triple on this hole today?" Instead of thinking about avoiding a big number on the hole, you need to take a success approach to the hole:

how are you going to hit quality shots on the hole? Break the hole down into separate shots: tee shot, approach shot, and putt. The goal then is to hit a quality tee shot, or better yet, hit a shot to the target. I call this "common denominator thinking." Each shot should be played independent of the next. For example, don't label the shot as "a tee shot on hole number 6 where I always make double." View the first shot as a shot you are trying to hit to an intended target without attaching any significance to score on the hole.

I often start a round well, but by the end of the round, my swing starts to break down and gets sloppy. I hate it when my swing comes unglued after I had a good round under way. How can I continue to score my best on the remaining holes?

You said the key word: *score*. Your mental error is focusing too much on the swing or breakdowns in the swing and not paying attention to getting the job done. You may get tired, swing faster, or guide your swing as you near the end of the round. In any case, you can't let a couple of bad shots steer you down the path of "playing golf swing."

- Abandon playing golf the "right way" for the "functional way." Put aside judgments about your golf swing and think about getting the ball in the hole any way you can. Don't try to fix the problem, either. This will probably make matters worse. At the most, use one swing cue (that has worked in the past) to help you get some tempo or feel back. Stick to the basics and don't search for a magical key that will fix your swing.

- Use your "go-to" shot to keep the ball in play. Hit the shot you are confident you can get into play. This may be a low cut or punch shot. Get the job done—and don't worry if it's not the shot you should play.

- Save your energy for the end of the round. Don't grind between shots by thinking intensely about your next shot. You can't possibly focus for four hours straight. Instead, relax your focus between shots and reserve your mental energy for the end of the round.

I have a tough time dealing with negative people on the golf course. Yesterday a person with a condescending and negative attitude got me off my game in an important tournament. How can I cope with this?

You obviously pay too much attention to what other members of your group are doing. First, don't get sucked into playing this person's mind game and get into a grudge match. If you bring yourself down to his or her level and use the same tactics, you've been drawn into destructive mental warfare. Second, it's up to you how you choose to respond to others in the group. The fact that this person is condescending is not the real issue, because you are not likely going to change another person's behavior. The real issue is how you react to this person. Negative comments, rudeness, or a general lack of respect toward you could be a psych-out tactic used by your playing partner. In that case, this person is achieving his or her intentions—to get you upset and disrupt your game. Don't dwell on such rudeness. It's best if you focus on what needs to be done to score well. For example, try to ignore what's going on around you by walking down the opposite side of the fairway. Pay attention to playing one shot at a time and going deeper into your golfing cocoon. Minor distractions become major ones only when you focus on them.

REFERENCES

Berglass, Steven (1986). *The Success Syndrome: Hitting Bottom When You Reach the Top.* Plenum Press: New York, NY.

Covey, Steven R. (1989). *The Seven Habits of Highly Effective People.* Fireside: New York, NY.

Geiberger, Al (1980). *Tempo: How to Find It and How to Keep It.* Golf Digest: Trumbull, CT.

INDEX

About the Author

Dr. Patrick Cohn heads Peak Performance Sports. A leading sport and golf psychologist, author, and professional speaker, Dr. Cohn teaches his methods to golfers on the PGA Tour, LPGA Tour, BUY.COM Tour, and Golden Bear Tour and to several collegiate and amateur players. Dr. Cohn earned a Ph.D. in sport psychology from the University of Virginia in 1991. Experts in sport psychology consider him the leading authority on preshot routines and putting psychology. Dr. Cohn's mental game programs were developed from more than a decade of work and research with world-class golfers. He is the author of *The Mental Game of Golf: A Guide to Peak Performance*, *Peak Performance Golf: How Good Golfers Become Great Ones*, and coauthor of *The Mental Art of Putting: Using Your Mind to Putt Your Best*. He stars in the audio book *Think to Win: How to Manage Your Mind on the Golf Course* and the video, *Make Your Most Confident Stroke: A Guide to a One-Putt Mindset* and costars in the audio *Great Putting—Right Now! Mental Keys to Confident Putting*. Dr. Cohn also teaches his sport psychology methods to PGA professionals, athletic trainers, and health care professionals. The PGA of America approves his education seminars for education credits. He has appeared twice as a special guest on The Golf Channel. He is also a regular columnist for Golfweb.com, and his articles have appeared in *Golf* magazine, *PGA* magazine, and *Golfweek*. Dr. Cohn works at Grand Cypress Resort in Orlando, Florida.

Contact Dr. Patrick Cohn at:
  Peak Performance Sports
  7380 Sand Lake Rd.
  Suite 500, PBM 5012
  Orlando, FL 32819
  Phone: 407-909-1700
  Toll-free: 888-742-7225
  E-mail: pcohn@peaksports.com
  Website: www.peaksports.com

Publications by Dr. Patrick Cohn

Peak Performance Golf: How Good Golfers Become Great Ones

For serious students of the game who are struggling to improve their overall performance, this unique guide teaches intermediate to advanced golfers how to get the most out of their abilities, prepare for competition, and lower their scores. Dr. Cohn teaches you how to develop a plan for practice, reach for your dreams, take care of your body, eat healthy foods, improve physical fitness, prepare your mind for play, and improve practice habits. Contemporary Books.
221 pages • $16.95 U.S.

The Mental Game of Golf: A Guide to Peak Performance

Written by Dr. Patrick Cohn, noted consultant to tour pros, *The Mental Game of Golf* teaches golfers how to master their mental game and play with greater confidence and composure. It combines the author's work, research, and tips from tour pros to illustrate the mental skills and routines needed to play well. Peak Performance Sports, 888-742-7225 or www.peaksports.com.
169 pages • $19.95 U.S.

The Mental Art of Putting: Using Your Mind to Putt Your Best

Written by Dr. Patrick Cohn and Robert Winters, M.A., *The Mental Art of Putting* is the first book that helps players master the mental side of putting. Based on their work and research with 20 of the greatest putters on tour, this book helps you to be confident, focused, and fearless on the green. You are given the keys to developing preshot routines, warm-up routines, and scoring better on the greens. Peak Performance Sports, 888-742-7225 or www.peaksports.com.
139 pages • $19.95 U.S.

Think To Win: How to Manage Your Mind on the Golf Course (Audio)

Read by Dr. Patrick Cohn, this two-tape audio program teaches golfers how to avoid self-sabotage and take their practice game to the course. This unique instruction program gives golfers field-tested practical strategies to help transfer their skills to the course, practice better, find the zone, and play with confidence, composure, and consistency. Peak Performance Sports, 888-742-7225 or www.peaksports.com.
2 audiotapes; 110 minutes • $18.95 U.S.

Great Putting—Right Now! Mental Keys to Confident Putting (Audio)

Read by Dr. Patrick Cohn and Robert Winters, M.A., two leading experts in putting psychology. Learn how to putt and think like a great putter and use the power of choice to be more confident and focused. Perfect for golfers who are streaky putters or players who struggle with putting! Peak Performance Sports, 888-742-7225 or www.peaksports .com.
1 audiotape; 74 minutes • $12.00 U.S.

Make Your Most Confident Stroke: A Guide to a One-Putt Mindset (Video)

Dr. Patrick Cohn and PGA Tour player Grant Waite give you the secrets to being confident, focused, and free on the greens. They show you how to develop a confident putting routine so you can focus on the task and make more putts. Drills for developing touch to eliminate three-putting are also included. Peak Performance Sports, 888-742-7225 or www.peak-sports.com.
1 video; 37 minutes • $22.95 U.S.

Peak Performance Golf Insights (Newsletter)

Edited by Dr. Patrick Cohn, *Peak Performance Golf Insights* includes feature articles on how to think better, recent research in sport psychology, and quotes from tour professionals. Each issue covers a different topic on how to apply sport psychology techniques to your golf game. Peak Performance Sports, 888-742-7225 or www.peaksports.com.
2 issues; Spring and Fall • $10 per one-year subscription